THE IMMIGRANT WAR

*****

"A good introduction to the subject of global migration. ... likely
to lead in controversial but potentially very stimulating directions"
Migrants Rights Network.

"Here is a book which truly takes forward the struggle for social
justice. Vittorio Longhi's comprehensive and vivid study reveals a
growing international movement that gets negligible coverage in
the mainstream press but yet which requires a radical rethink of
dominant approaches to immigration, development and democracy.
'The immigrant war' introduces us to a new generation of migrants
who will shape the world in aftermath of neo-liberalism."
Hilary Wainwright, Transnational Institute, and co-editor of Red Pepper

"As much an exercise in the continued value of anti-capitalist
theory, as a monograph of an emerging class, struggling for
survival. One can't help but walk away from Longhi's book feeling
gripped by its raw conceptual binaries: hierarchy versus equality,
exploitation versus unions, Europe versus the global south."
Souicant

"A convincing case that the labour conditions of all workers
cannot be improved without understanding and addressing the
problems faced by migrant workers. *The Immigrant War* adds greatly
to our understanding of those problems."
Counterfire

"This book's greatest virtue, and the places where Longhi really
becomes an eloquent advocate himself, is in the descriptions of
how all over the world migrants are organizing and fighting for
their rights. That's the true hope for the future."
Truthout

"One of the most insightful books ever written on global
migration patterns and their consequences from a humane
perspective. A must read."
Devendra Dhungana, UNDP's Livelihood Recovery for Peace Project

*****

THE IMMIGRANT WAR

A global movement against
discrimination and exploitation

Vittorio Longhi

Translated from original Italian by Janet Eastwood

First published in Great Britain in 2014 by

The Policy Press
University of Bristol
6th Floor
Howard House
Queen's Avenue
Bristol BS8 1SD
UK
Tel +44 (0)117 331 5020
Fax +44 (0)117 331 5367
e-mail tpp-info@bristol.ac.uk
www.policypress.co.uk

North American office:
The Policy Press
c/o The University of Chicago Press
1427 East 60th Street
Chicago, IL 60637, USA
t: +1 773 702 7700
f: +1 773-702-9756
e:sales@press.uchicago.edu
www.press.uchicago.edu

The translation of this work has been funded by SEPS

SEGRETARIATO EUROPEO PER LE PUBBLICAZIONI SCIENTIFICHE

Via Val d'Aposa 7 - 40123 Bologna - Italy
seps@seps.it - www.seps.it

British Library Cataloguing in Publication Data
A catalogue record for this book is available from the British Library

Library of Congress Cataloging-in-Publication Data
A catalog record for this book has been requested

ISBN 978 1 44730 589 7 paperback

Cover design by Qube Design Associates
Front cover: photograph kindly supplied by Matilde Gattoni
Printed and bound in Great Britain by Short Run Press, Exeter

Contents

PREFACE

The war

'The de facto apartheid that I witnessed in this rundown district was only one episode in a relentless war against illegal immigration that is beginning to recall some of the darker periods of European history.' The place Matthew Carr[1] is referring to in this article for the *New York Times* is Attiki Square in Athens, where families of migrants and refugees, particularly Afghans, gather, who are regularly attacked by Greek neo-Nazi groups and then made to move on by the police.

When I read the article I was struck by the title 'The war against immigrants' and the way Carr linked the stories of manhunts in various parts of Europe and the Mediterranean. 'I have seen French police in Calais confiscate blankets from homeless migrants in what one official described to me as a "cleaning operation". I have seen starving Somali migrants in Greece rummaging through rubbish bins; Afghan asylum seekers in France hunted down by police in abandoned railway sidings; penniless Malians living in ruined buildings in southern Spain; and African migrants hiding from police raids in the forests of Morocco.'

These are stories of migration, which recur and resemble each other, just like the actions by police on the border all inevitably recall military operations, planned and coordinated as though in a real conflict, faced with a 'real enemy'. It should be clear by now that economic migration is a physiological mobility phenomenon, linked in particular to the demand for labour in advanced economies and the globalisation process and the revolution in communication and transport. And managing this phenomenon requires multilateral agreements and coordination by international institutions, with clear and shared rules. Instead, migration has been left to single governments' policies that are influenced by domestic propaganda

---

[1] Carr, M. (2010) 'The war against immigrants', *New York Times, La Repubblica*, 8 November.

reasons, portraying this phenomenon as a temporary event to be contained, or in the worst cases, as a threat to local identity and the security of their own citizens. For this reason governments all tend to militarise their borders, greatly restricting entry and limiting as much as possible the duration of permits to stay.

This approach and these policies have created a new, obvious contradiction between the need for foreign workers in advanced economies and the possibility of entering, living and working legally with dignity. Excessive restrictions do not stop movements, but make them more insecure, contribute to creating illegality and expose thousands of people to trafficking, exploitation and the risk of death. This is happening in every flow of migrants today and it is happening every day: from Africa and the Middle East to Europe, from South East Asia to the Persian Gulf or Australia and from Central America to the United States.

The conflict evoked by the *New York Times* article does not stop at borders, however; it reaches to the heart of social life, penetrating and permeating economic relations and the political and cultural sphere of the countries of destination. Even when someone does succeed in crossing a border, even when they obtain a permit and find a steady job, they are still faced with this 'implacable war' against migrants. Historically the worst jobs with the hardest working conditions and the least pay are reserved for immigrants. They also have to face xenophobic propaganda that is so functional to what Michel Foucault would call 'biopower',[2] or the 'subjugation of bodies and the control of populations'.

The immigrant war examines four migration routes from which appear, on the one hand, continuous, indiscriminate abuse suffered by foreigners: violence against Asians in the richest countries of the Persian Gulf, attacks against Central Americans without documents in the US, the ghettoisation of people from the Middle East in France and the exploitation of Africans in Italy. In these same contexts, on the other hand, all the migrants' potential for conflict and to make

---

[2] See Foucault, M. (1997) *Il faut défendre la société* [*Society must be defended*], Paris: Hautes Etudes Seuil–Gallimard.

demands comes to the surface, as they change from being passive victims to become new, conscious social agents, capable of fighting for their own rights and contributing to the revival of a wider protest.

Noam Chomsky wrote that for some time we have been witnessing an 'international assault on labor',[3] referring to the processes of de-unionisation, flexibilisation and deregulation of the right to work. In the eternal conflict between capital and labour, the arguments of capital and the market have prevailed also in those countries that founded their constitutions on rights and social protection, necessary elements for development, cohesion and democracy. According to US linguist Chomsky, there is a new 'precarious proletariat' today, which includes those traditionally on the margins of the labour market, such as migrants, and those who until now lived under conditions of greater stability, protection and opportunity; the current assault on labour is not even sparing young people in industrialised countries, the locals. In our knowledge economy, we now have a whole generation living in frustration and uncertainty, because of casual work and general insecurity, and because of spreading unemployment in the absence of former protection.

Migrants and casual young workers are not two separate aspects of the labour market, two contrasting elements, even opposed in some cases, as one might think. Instead they are united by the same structural conditions of insecurity and vulnerability. I argue that the same unity should be found to fight back against the system, aiming for a political reassembling of the various forms of resistance[4] and for the creation of a 'collective will' that the Marxist thinker Antonio Gramsci[5] used to cry out for.

The protests that took place in 2011, from the Arab Spring, to the movements of the Spanish indignados in Europe, and to the Occupy Wall Street demonstrations in the US, show how dissatisfied this

[3] Chomsky, N. (2011) 'The international assault on labor', Truthout, 4 May (www.truth-out.org/internationl-assault-labor/1304431702).
[4] Mezzadra, S. and Negri A. (2011) 'Lotte di classe e ricomposizione politica nella crisi' ['The struggles of class and the recomposition of society in the crisis'], UniNomade, 12 January.
[5] Gramsci, A. (1975) Quaderni dal carcere [Prison notebooks], vol 3, Turin: Einaudi, pp 1055-6.

generation is with the current economic and political system, how the level of social injustice has become insupportable. For the very same reasons, a new consciousness is spreading among migrant workers, who are responding to attacks by rebelling against humiliation and segregation, and taking part in demonstrations, protests and strikes. They are using new tools for communication – blogs and online social networks – and, with the support of anti-racist movements, trade unions and non-government organisations, in many cases they are succeeding in winning important battles and influencing the policies of governments, restoring respect for migrants' fundamental rights. A global movement against discrimination and exploitation seems to be taking shape, albeit in a spontaneous, diverse and uncoordinated way. This movement may be connected to the multitude wanting to restore dignity to labour and a future to new generations, migrants and locals together.

1

In the Persian Gulf

Return from hell

First the passengers get off. Hundreds of Nepalis returning home, dragging trolleys and big, heavy bags. Small groups of Western tourists who have arrived in Kathmandu with backpacks and trekking boots, stand out among them. Only at the end are large, anonymous wooden boxes seen appearing, which are unloaded slowly from the 747s of Qatar Airways or Air India and accompanied on trolleys to the exit. On average two coffins arrive at Tribhuvan International Airport every day. They are bringing back the bodies of migrants, who went to work as bricklayers, workmen or drivers, but in particular as domestic servants, in the rich countries of the Middle East, the Persian Gulf or East Asia. The families wait outside, almost always in silence. They have already wept for a long time for the children, wives, husbands, sisters or brothers, whose bodies remained for months in those countries' mortuaries, before the local authorities gave permission to bring them back home. The coffins are unloaded one by one, as usually happens with coffins from military aircraft. In this case, however, there are no flags covering the bare boxes, no parades and no state funerals. There are no politicians or television cameras. These deaths no longer make the news and now there is only a daily ritual that recurs in general indifference. In fact every family quickly loads the box onto the luggage rack of a small Toyota van, almost as though they are embarrassed by the tragic conclusion of a journey that was started full of hope, and hurry away from the airport, disappearing into the Kathmandu valley.

Nepali migrants die for different reasons, even though the stories often coincide. The medical report accompanying the body of Bimala BK[1] in April 2011 stated that she had committed suicide five months earlier.[2] Her family knew she had been mistreated but never thought she would return in a coffin. Bimala was 31 years old and had left

1

the district of Udayapur in Eastern Nepal in September 2009 for Kuwait, where she had found work as a home help. Waiting for her at Tribhuvan Airport was not her husband, who had already gone to Malaysia, where he had remarried, but her son Roshan, along with her three young sisters aged 7, 12 and 14. Mani Kumar Subba, who was also a domestic servant, died in Saudi Arabia in 2009. It took his wife Karuna four months of continuous requests to the Ministry for Foreign Affairs and the employment agency that had taken him on, to get the body back.[3] According to the agency, Mani had been found dead in a swimming pool, and in these cases obtaining permission to send the body back takes time. "What will I say to your children? How can your children go on?" sobs the niece of Lila Aachraya, 29 years old, as the box leaves the airport.[4] Lila had gone to Lebanon through an agency that had promised her decent work with a family, but she soon found herself forced to work impossible hours and suffered physical abuse. "She had asked the agency to return home, but the middlemen wanted 2,800 dollars and we couldn't afford it," recounts her niece. "They threatened to kill her, then no more communication for weeks, until the news of her death."

According to the Nepalese embassy, from January to October 2011, 13 migrant workers committed suicide, 22 work-related deaths were documented and 92 deaths were unexplained.[5] The *Kathmandu Post* estimates that in Saudi Arabia, for example, about 30 Nepalis die every month and that 3,200 workers have died from 2000 to 2012.[6] Officially they die due to accidents, particularly on building sites, road accidents or heart attacks. But a large proportion are homicides and suicides, particularly among women, because of the sexual abuse and harassment they suffer from their employers. "Fatalities relating to migrant employment are usually taken for granted because of their high number," comments the Nepali journalist Devendra Dhungana.[7] Part of the responsibility, he adds, is due to lack of control by the authorities: "Job advertisements in newspapers are not verified properly and thugs are making the most of the grey areas. Officials at the Department of Labour are also influenced by these people."

An official from the Ministry for Foreign Affairs, Pushpa Bhattarai, prefers to attribute the cause of death to heart attacks. These happen particularly at night, while asleep, because 'Nepalis are not prepared for the suffocating temperatures of the countries of the Gulf and passing quickly from extreme heat to strong air conditioning may be fatal.'[8] As for road accidents, Nepalis are victims of dangerous driving, particularly in the Middle East, because they are knocked down while crossing the road or because they are hit by cars. Suicide and homicide are attributed to depression and the great stress involved in working abroad and returning home. The government believes that they should, therefore, provide more information and more training, including languages, to workers before they move, so that they are able to better adjust to the conditions they find in countries that are so different. However, while it is true that many leave without knowing what awaits them, it is difficult to say whether training really could make a difference. A Nepali migrant returning home in a coffin represents not only sorrow for the family, but also a source of income that has been cut off. And even if families succeed in getting a body back for cremation, after months of bureaucratic procedures at embassies and employment offices, there remains the problem of collecting back pay and compensation from insurance companies, which requires just as much time and effort.

The Nepali authorities attribute these difficulties to lack of protection for their fellow citizens in the countries of destination, particularly those in the Gulf, aggravated by a form of discrimination against non-Muslim foreigners and those coming from developing countries. In 2010 almost a million people emigrated from Nepal, about 3 per cent of the population. The majority were workers with few qualifications, who were in debt or had sold land and property to pay employment agencies acting as brokers, hoping to find respectable employment abroad. In March 2012 the Ministry of Labour tried to introduce reforms to prevent abuses by employment agencies and to highlight the systemic corruption of government officials, but with little result.

Official estimates in 2011 talk of about three million Nepali emigrants, but they could even be double that in reality, because so many don't have documents and there is no control of anyone moving to countries such as India, where the border is practically open. In 2011 remittances from migrants brought about four billion dollars into the country, equal to 20 per cent of the gross domestic product

(GDP).[9] According to the classification by The World Bank in 2010,[10] Nepal was in sixth place among nations depending on remittances from immigrants, coming after Tajikistan, Lesotho, Moldavia, the islands of Samoa, and the Kyrgyz Republic.

Immigration sociologists now agree on the progressive feminisation of migrant work and Nepal's reality fully confirms this: 68 out of 100 migrants are women. They are the ones now actively supporting their families and are therefore part of the national economy. Nevertheless, these 'global women', as the US writer Barbara Erhenreich described them,[11] continue to be those most exposed to physical, sexual and psychological abuse. In Kuwait, for example, violence is so widespread that the embassy has had to take over a building to accommodate domestic servants running away from abusive masters of the house, who often withhold their documents and pay for months. In every case the fate of Nepali women is no different from that of other migrants from South West Asia. The brutality with which Sri Lankan, Bangladeshi, Filipino or Indonesian women are treated in rich Eastern countries is the same and recurs endlessly, with almost complete impunity.

The story of the Sri Lankan home help L.P. Ariyawathie, 49 years old, who in August 2010 escaped from Saudi Arabia because of the torture inflicted on her by the master of the house, was known all over the world.[12] No sooner had she disembarked at Colombo, Sri Lanka, than she was taken immediately to Kamburupitiya Hospital because she could no longer walk or sit without pain. X-rays showed that 24 nails had been driven into her body. "The nails are about 5 centimetres long and are in her arms and legs in particular, there is even one on her forehead under the skin," explained the hospital director to journalists. From the capital the employment office said it wanted to start an inquiry and the Minister for Foreign Affairs, G.L. Peiris, requested clarification from the Saudi ambassador. But from Riyadh the government, the Chamber of Commerce and other institutional representatives responded immediately, denying what the woman had said and accusing her of inventing it all to extort money. Mrs Ariyawathie recounted in detail how the torture took place: "It was inflicted by the master of the house with a hammer, almost always in the evening, while the other members of the family around used to laugh."[13] Amnesty International wrote to the Saudi Minister of Justice, Mohammed bin Abdul Aziz al-Issa, to ask him to investigate the facts and any responsibility by the police, to find out if anyone else knew of the matter. Amnesty also asked for the case to be brought to court according to international regulations and for compensation to be paid to the victim. So far, however, only Sri Lanka's authorities have acted to support the Ariyawathie family, providing her and her daughter with the means to go on. Notwithstanding the declared intentions of the authorities, it remains to be seen what the law can really do in a case like this, considering the economic dependence on remittances from the Gulf countries. In 2010 Sri Lanka had 18 million workers abroad[14] – 70 per cent of them women – creating over US$4 billion of wealth for the country.[15]

On this subject, the story of Nour Miyati, the Indonesian domestic servant who in 2005 succeeded in taking her Saudi employers to court for serious mistreatment, is symbolic.[16] Nour, 25 years old, had been tied up for a month and left for days without food, until the family had to take her to hospital. She was treated for dehydration and malnutrition and gangrene in her foot, the toes of which had to be amputated. Despite the evidence and the admission by the master of the house, the judge initially accused the domestic servant of false testimony and sentenced her to 79 lashes. Nour's lawyers got a new trial, thanks to pressure from the US non-governmental organisation (NGO) Human Rights Watch, and in 2008 a judge in Riyadh granted her compensation of just US$670, without any sentence against the Saudi couple. Activists from the US NGO called the sentence 'scandalous', accusing the judges of giving a 'very dangerous' message to employers in this way, because it authorised them to beat their domestic servants with complete impunity, while the victims had no hope of getting justice. Cases of abuse and mistreatment continued, but in 2011, after formal protests by the Indonesian President, Susilo Bambang Yudhoyono, the Saudi government decided to close the borders to workers coming from Jakarta.[17] The same kind of retaliation had already been carried out against Filipino domestic workers following accusations of abuse and rape and denouncements by the authorities in Manila. The Filipino government had established a series of regulations for its domestic workers, with a minimum wage, social security and requirements for accommodation.[18] In reality the Saudis took advantage of this to open the market to Bangladeshi immigrants, who were prepared to take US$170 dollars a month, less than half of what had been imposed by Manila.

During a mission in the Gulf in April 2010 the United Nations (UN) Commissioner for Human Rights, Navanethem Pillay, quoted studies and research showing 'illegal practises of confiscating passports, withholding salaries and exploitation by unscrupulous employment agencies'.[19] Notwithstanding appreciation for legal improvements in some countries, 'the situation of migrant domestic workers is particularly worrying,' she added, drawing attention to the fact that these workers often 'do not have the possibility of turning to the law'.

Who built the country?

The dynamics of economic migration to the region of the Persian Gulf have no equal in the international context. This is a relatively recent story, following first the development of the oil sector and then the development of infrastructure and services. The six major Arab countries of the region are associated in the Cooperation Council for the Arab States of the Gulf (CCG), the organisation that was set up in 1981 to create a common market.[20] Bahrain, Kuwait, Oman, Qatar, Saudi Arabia and the United Arab Emirates have experienced very similar economic events and, as for migration, today they are the countries attracting the greatest number of foreign workers in the world, on whom they effectively depend. Here also the contradiction between the need for migrants and the way they are treated and forced to live appears most clearly. The contradiction is even greater, when you think that the number of immigrants is more than double the local population.

Flows of migrants followed various phases in the history of the region. Even at the end of 1930, when oil was found in the area, specialist workers started arriving from neighbouring countries, first from Iran and India, then also from Yemen, Egypt, Syria and Palestine.[21] Until the early 1970s the total number of migrants was still small, about 800,000, and the balance between the import and export of the labour force was essentially positive, especially for Iraq and Oman. Historians and economists agree that the turning point came in 1973, when the Arab States belonging to the Organisation of Petrol Exporting Countries (OPEC) decided to cut off supplies to Europe and the United States. This was in retaliation for the support given to Israel in the Yom Kippur War against Syria and Egypt.[22] The cost of crude oil tripled and a period of energy crisis started, which hit European countries in particular, at least until 1975. The producers in the Gulf, a small group of monarchs and landowners, started to earn money as never before, and this boom needed an ever increasing number of workers, who continued to come from other Arab States and to a small extent from Asia, in particular India, Pakistan and Sri Lanka. A new rise in the price of crude oil in 1979 subsequently made the oil states rich, driving them to spend on infrastructure, services and welfare intended for the local population. Anthropologist Ahmed Kanna recalls that before the oil boom there were progressive political forces opposed to autocratic monarchies in those states, such as the anti-corporation movements in Saudi Arabia, the Marxist National Liberation Front in Bahrain and Oman and the National Front in Dubai. 'From the 70s Qatar, Kuwait, the Emirates and to some extent Saudi Arabia succeeded in avoiding any kind of popular political formation, thanks to oil and demographic trends,'[23] with the exception of Bahrain, which has few natural resources. With the wealth derived from oil, explains Kanna, a welfare and social security system was created, in which there was no longer room for demands and all labouring work was transferred to migrants. In fact the number of foreigners tripled in 10 years, reaching 44 million in 1985 (although the total number was much higher, considering families were being reunited).

At the same time the increase in prices and small number of inhabitants clearly transformed the six small countries of the Gulf into *rentier* states,[24] since 80 per cent of public income and in some cases even more came from the wells, allowing governments to live from revenue without taxing the citizens.[25] To redistribute so much wealth more and more jobs were created in the public sector, but strictly reserved for the locals, with high wages and privileges. This resulted in a dual labour market with the Arabs of the Gulf in well-paid public employment on the one hand, and foreigners in heavy labour or badly paid work in the private sector on the other hand. Two markets and two social classes – citizens and non-citizens, bourgeoisie and proletariat, to use a 20th-century model – without any prospect of integration or mobility, with migrants being perceived and represented as potential threats to the culture, values and identity of the locals.[26]

At the end of the 1980s oil revenue started to decrease, while major infrastructure works were going ahead and a new generation of qualified local workers was growing up. Notwithstanding clearly nationalistic labour policies, jobs available in the public sector grew scarce, and the young people of the Gulf were now too qualified to accept manual jobs in the private sector. As a result, the level of national unemployment reached about 20 per cent in the course of 10 years, while the number of migrants employed did not stop going up. The historical events of these years contributed to the new composition of the foreign labour force. The 1991 Gulf War caused an exodus from the region of about 1.5 million Egyptians, Yemenis, Palestinians and Jordanians, who were considered problematic politically and potential supporters of the Iraqi regime. To replace them came workers from South East Asia, from the ex-Soviet Republics after the fall of the Berlin Wall, and more recently from East Africa. At the end of the 1990s, migrants arriving, who were predominantly employed in the construction industry, domestic work, services and tourism, reached more than 7 million, equal to 70 per cent of the labour force in the CCG area. The latest estimates say that they exceed 10 million, with a local population of about 6 million.[27]

The most striking thing, even today, is the contrast between the double standard of living and wealth, apart from the system of segregation and the impossibility of any kind of integration. An investigation by the International Trade Union Confederation (ITUC) contrasts the annual per capita income of a citizen of Qatar, about US$88,000, with the highest pay to which a Nepali worker could aspire, about US$3,600 a year. A Filipino domestic worker never exceeds US$2,500 a year for an up-to-18-hour day.[28] The imbalance is even more apparent in the organisation of the city, between the luxury of the skyscrapers, hotels and large shopping centres reserved for the locals and foreign tourists on the one hand, and the poverty of the work camps on the other, where the mainly Asiatic migrants live. The camps are ghettos confined to the outskirts on dirt roads, where great hives with few services rise up, squalid, overcrowded dormitories where companies accommodate migrants, almost all of them male. One of the most well known is in Muhaisnah in Dubai, which everyone calls Sonapur and which ironically means 'city of gold' in Hindi. It rose up between a rubbish dump and an old cemetery. More than 150,000 workers live there. "These are the people who built the country, transformed the desert into beautiful cities and now they have to live like this," says Saaed, a Pakistani driver, while passing through the camp from which the towers of Dubai in the gleaming bank quarter may be seen in the distance.[29]

The social exclusion, terrible living conditions and abuse reserved for migrants are also possible thanks to the entry quota mechanism. So far in the six states permits to stay have been regulated according to the criterion of *kafala* (sponsorship), which binds the migrant to a short-term contract with a sole employer. He is financially and legally responsible for the employee for the duration of the contract as well as having the power to withhold the migrant's passport and suspend payment of his salary, binding him exclusively to the employer on penalty of loss of permit and immediate repatriation. In Saudi Arabia and Kuwait employers may also prevent people leaving the country freely. It is a system that makes even a minimum form of integration and social mobility impossible in a context that is already extremely closed to expatriate workers.[30] In a report on Qatar, the US State Department wrote that 'sponsorship rules may lead to forced labour activities under conditions of slavery',[31] while for the International Labour Organization (ILO) *kafala* 'causes distortions in the labour market and may fuel trafficking in human beings'.[32]

Governments may have started to discuss this system due to international pressures. In August 2009 Bahrain made liberal reforms to the regulations on permits, allowing migrants to change employer simply by giving three months' notice, encouraging mobility and removing the risk of passports being confiscated. According to Mohammed Dito, Vice President of the Labour Market Regulatory Authority (LMRA) of Bahrain, "the real problem with *kafala* is the way access is gained to the labour market, because now it is companies and individual employers, who own the permits to stay".[33] The permit should be managed by the state instead, he says, not delegated to private individuals, who have "excessive power and total control over the worker" in this way.

Kafala apart, however, it must be considered that some rights and fundamental protection do not apply, not even for the citizens of the Gulf themselves. Of the CCG governments, only Kuwait has ratified the two conventions of the ILO on freedom of association and the right to collective bargaining.[34] Notwithstanding this, in Kuwait, as in other countries, a single trade union system is in force, which allows effective control by the government. In Saudi Arabia and the Arab Emirates the formation of free trade unions, and going on strike, is not allowed.[35] There are minor forms of association, such as workers' committees, but only in some sectors and in companies with a certain number of employees, where bargaining is very restricted. None of this concerns migrants. "There will be no equality and parity of treatment between locals and immigrants until we have complete respect for the basic regulations, which protect the right to work, from freedom of association to the rejection of discrimination," comments Khalil Bohazza, a Bahraini journalist and blogger.

Faced with such a scenario, why do foreigners, who are also in the majority compared with the local population, not rebel and fight to demand equal treatment, at least from an employment point of view? Some scholars maintain that migrants find it difficult to organise themselves. Apart from a lack of bargaining power and lack of democratic spaces, for Jane Bristol Rhys[36] the level of division between workers must be taken into account. Some communities, such as the Indians, Egyptians and Pakistanis, reproduce structural hierarchies in the Gulf, which divide the societies of the countries they come from. 'Labour policies and practices in the Emirate seem to have reinforced class divisions within communities of immigrants, rather than developing transnational identities, taking no account of where they come from,' Bristol Rhys observes. Other researchers have a quite opposite view: 'Religious or caste differences play an insignificant part in this context of segregation, including the tensions between Hindus and Muslims, which have completely disappeared here,' says Andrew Gardner. Difficult living conditions and work rates do not leave time or energy for certain questions. 'Politics is a luxury we cannot afford here,' says an Indian interviewed by Gardner.[37]

Regarding the capacity of migrants in the Gulf to make demands, another aspect must be considered. There is a new generation of locals, who have been liberated from conservative, tribal systems and who are starting to be critical of their governments. They are discontented and frustrated because they are excluded from a labour market that does not offer any prospects and is still rigidly divided between an elite of locals and a mass of immigrants. In the region with the highest average per capita income in the world they are starting to feel the same tensions as the young Maghrebis of the Arab Spring. This is shown by the protests for democracy in Bahrain, which were organised by young people, including many from the middle class.

The demand for rights and freedom by this generation is not different or separate from the demand for decent work by migrants; in fact it complements it. It arises from the same structure based on privilege, exclusion and conflict, now not only between locals and migrants but also between two generations of workers and citizens. According to the political analyst Adam Hanieh, however, for foreigners in this area to be involved in the fight for democracy there really needs to be transnational coordination. "It is very important for trade union movements in the whole area of the Middle East to be well connected to each other and act to defend the rights of migrants, but unfortunately this has not been the priority of the trade unions and progressive organisations in the region so far."[38]

A time bomb

Prashant approaches the trade unionist's car smiling. He is happy because the last two refrigerators have just been delivered to the Haji Hassan work camp. One fridge for every two rooms, making one for every 10 people. "It's a good result," he says, "for us who live here." The heat of summer reaches unbearable levels and there is no other way of keeping the food the workers buy on the market outside the gates of the camp, with everything laid out on two carpets on the ground, which is on a dust road between sheds and housing on the outskirts of Manama in Bahrain.

Prashant comes from Rajasthan, and for 10 years he has worked for Hassan, the largest construction group in the country, which controls 16 companies and has about 1,800 employees, 300 of whom are locals and 1,500 migrants. Prashant was one of the first 200 foreigners to become a member of the company trade union, which was formed in 2006. He recounts with pride how he took part in the 2007 strike for salary increases and for less crowded rooms, with air conditioning and refrigerators. This was the first dispute in the building sector dedicated entirely to migrants, which was supported and organised by the Trade Union Federation of Bahrain, GFBTU. "We made our delegates understand that, if they put forward a case to improve living conditions in concrete terms and increase the salaries of foreign workers, they would actively take part in the organisation," explains Abdulla Hussain, the GFBTU representative, who followed the dispute.[39]

It was not easy to begin with, as the workers were afraid of 'sticking their necks out' and making demands; they were afraid of losing their jobs and being sent home. There was also a language problem, because they all came from different countries: Nepal, India, Pakistan and Sri Lanka. In fact many companies deliberately diversified the composition of the labour force, based on nationality, to prevent groups of workers forming that were too united. Negotiations continued for six months after the first demands to Hassan's management, but the company continued to maintain that they were standard conditions and it would not consider other costs. At that point the trade union proposed a strike, and after some initial resistance the migrants accepted. When the company buses went to pick them up from the camp and take them to the building sites, more than 1,600 refused to leave and stayed on the camp for a whole day, 24 consecutive hours. "The management called us immediately, saying that the company was prepared to negotiate," recalls Hussain. Increases of ten dinars a month (about US$26) were agreed, accommodation was thinned out, from 9 to 5 people to a room, air conditioning was installed and the supply of refrigerators ensured. Above all, however, the workers had shown that with well-coordinated and united action they could really change conditions, and this drove another 900 migrants to register with the trade union immediately, recording almost total membership. But there was no shortage of retaliations. During the dispute the company suspended trade unions' fees by one dinar a month for each employee, and after the strike it closed the delegates' office.[40] The new union structure then tried to form a federation with the trade union of a company controlled by Haji Hassan, Precast Concrete, but the management prevented it. If they had succeeded in having a trade union federation in the building industry, say the workers, they could have asked for the harmonisation of wages in the various companies, which would have given workers much more bargaining power. Most of these workers, just like at Hassan, are migrants, and represent over 77 per cent of the workforce in Bahrain.

The GFBTU formally arose as a federation in 2004, after the law of 2002 recognised freedom of association. The current leaders, Abdulla Hussain and Karim Radhi, had operated underground for years since the 1970s, when the organisation was considered illegal. Today the federation has about 60 affiliated organisations, even though in the small kingdom of Bahrain bargaining is only allowed at company level and there are no national agreements. This is without doubt the country of the Gulf where there is a minimum of trade union freedom and collective bargaining, although with many restrictions and although the relevant international conventions have still not been ratified. In the past few years the government has also started down the route of social dialogue following the ILO's tripartite model, with the participation of companies, trade unions and the Ministry for Employment.

The leaders and members of the GFBTU were among the protagonists in the popular protest for democratic reforms in the spring of 2011, which had Pearl Square in the centre of Manama as its symbolic location and followed the wave of demonstrations, starting in Tunisia and spreading through Egypt and Libya, leading to the fall of lengthy dictatorships. The Al-Khalifa Sunni monarchy accused the Shi'ite members of the population of stirring up revolts, and aired the theory of outside support, from Iran in particular, to bring down the regime. I maintain that the need for change, however, takes no account of religious divisions, and is based on important questions of democracy and development, concerning Shi'ites and Sunnis in equal measure.

"We openly supported the initial demand for a new constitution, which would change the electoral system and put an end to economic inequality, including through the ratification of international agreements, but we never said we wanted to bring down the regime," said the General Secretary of the GFBTU, Salman Jaffar Al Mahfood.[41] The federation called a general strike on 15 March 2011 against the militarisation of the city and the violence against demonstrators and workers. The only reply was the government's dismissal of over 3,000 workers, who were also members of the trade union, for disciplinary reasons, which means that they were not even allowed access to unemployment benefit. Dozens of those whom the police had seen taking part in peaceful demonstrations in Pearl Square were also arrested. "The social dialogue in Bahrain was halted by the political crisis in 2011 and the trade union is no longer consulted, while companies are sticking close to the government," commented Al Mahfood.

More than a year later in Manama, the tension as a result of the clashes could still be felt in the continuous roadblocks along the streets leading to the centre and the police cordons around Pearl Square. The violence used to repress the demonstrations in the spring of 2011 drew criticism from the international community, particularly the US, which has military and financial interests on the island. King Hamad bin Hissa Al-Khalifa was therefore forced to agree to an independent commission of inquiry into violations of human rights. The Bahrain Independent Commission of Inquiry (BICI) presented a report, confirming unjustified arrests, the disproportionate use of force and torture. The toll was heavy: 35 confirmed dead, including 13 victims of clashes with the police and 5 victims of torture attributable to the Ministry for the Interior. Dozens disappeared and about 200 were arrested by national security agencies.[42] Another worrying fact also appears from the report, concerning the communities of Indian, Pakistani and Bangladeshi migrants who were subject to 'ethnic pogroms', violent attacks by xenophobic groups out of control. Four people were killed in cold blood. 'A band armed with steel bars and knives attacked some Pakistanis in a house in the Naeem area, some succeeded in escaping, but those who didn't were beaten to death,'[43] says the report. What exacerbated the climate of hostility towards foreigners in particular was the decision by the government to take on thousands of Pakistanis to reinforce internal forces, offering them salaries seven times more than those normally reserved for migrants, a move that clearly succeeded in dividing and opposing workers.[44]

"How can we go on like this? How sustainable is such a system in the long term? Under these conditions migrants are a time bomb, more dangerous than a nuclear bomb for the countries of the Gulf, if they do not make a start on reforms."[45] These are strong words by Majid Al Alawi, the ex-Minister for Employment of Bahrain. Al Alawi was in office for almost 10 years, from 2002 to 2011, until the explosion of protests. He prefers not to comment on the reasons for the revolt and the brutality with which it was put down, but the fact that he is no longer part of the executive already speaks volumes. Having lived for about 20 years in the United Kingdom and having worked in an international context, as a minister he introduced important innovations regarding admission policies and working conditions. Minimum salaries were increased and measures were adopted against the sale of temporary visas with greater control. "The objective was to create an internal labour market for foreigners," explains Al Alawi, "and in particular to reduce the distance between local workers and migrants." It was also during his mandate that the government reconsidered the system of *kafala*, allowing foreign workers to change employer by giving notice of just three months. However, the regulations were cancelled by the new restrictions of 2011 under the pretext of security. The government has restored the limits for giving notice to 15 months, discouraging any mobility in this way.

According to Al Alawi, "There is another fundamental question being faced today, in Bahrain as in the other countries of the Gulf, because expatriates are no longer only unskilled workers, but also professionals." The problem is that there is no social or cultural integration and there are still too many ghettos. "We must start to ask ourselves whether these are really temporary contracted workers or whether they are migrant workers and establish what kind of life plan lies behind their move. These young people are spending the best years of their life here, continually renewing short-term contracts and putting up with terrible conditions," maintains the ex-minister. "How can a situation of this kind really be considered temporary?" This view goes beyond measures to give work more dignity, and concerns the more delicate question of citizenship. "We must decide whether to establish a five-year limit to temporary work, which is not renewable in the same country. Or whether to proceed with naturalisation after this period."

The time bomb evoked by Al Alawi might not refer just to migrants, however. The protests in 2011 show that the new Bahraini generation is also unhappy with the system created by their fathers, a system based on inequality and on veiled authoritarianism. Beyond the repression of King Al-Khalifa, with a majority of foreign workers who have been kept in conditions of exclusion for a long time and a growing number of young people wishing for some radical changes, it seems that the time has come to rethink the entire political and social system, not just in the small kingdom of Bahrain, but in the whole region.

The trade union bridge

One of the most effective strategies the trade unions have developed in the last few years to influence working conditions and protect migrants in the Gulf and the Middle East has been working together with other unions, particularly when they have succeeded in building a 'bridge' between the organisations of the countries of origin and those in the places of destination. The aim is to follow and assist every migrant from departure to arrival. And on return.

R. Chandrasekharan is the head of the INTUC (Indian trade union confederation) of Kerala, the state that exports the most workers from India, more than four million throughout the world. He has a long experience in international organisations and has worked at cooperation projects with trade unions in receiving countries. In 2009 he started to work with the GFBTU of Bahrain. The project envisaged two phases for training workers: one before departure to become familiar with the contractual aspects and ways of obtaining assistance from Indian organisations and trade unions, the other immediately after arrival in Bahrain to adjust to the country, the culture, the way to behave and in particular the work they were going to be doing, health and safety conditions and rights.

"We want to reinforce these alliances in the region and are sure we will soon get other results, even if there are countries like Saudi Arabia, where we still meet great resistance," said the trade unionist.[46] The INTUC is also trying to establish agreements with other organisations in the Emirates. Even before arriving in another country, however, the main risk for Indians is falling into the clutches of private middlemen, real traffickers, often fellow countrymen, who have no hesitation in cheating them, promising non-existent jobs after the payment of thousands of dollars for visas. Some of these same middlemen then launder money made illegally, investing in emerging sectors of the economy of Kerala, such as tourism. Going along the coast south of Goa, you keep coming across resorts and Ayurvedic centres for rich Western tourists, where the logic of exploitation does not change: "a large part of the staff come from the countryside, salaries do not exceed US$50 a month and they depend almost exclusively on tips from clients, without any possibility of demanding better conditions," recounts Santhosh, a taxi driver and political activist from Chowara.

One of the greatest challenges remains that of getting migrant labour to go through public channels using legal means. Chandrasekharan explains that since 1996 there has been a state agency, the Non-Resident Keralites' Affairs Department (NORKA), which deals with assistance to residents abroad and allows constant monitoring of their work situation, including through embassies. Since contracts rarely provide for the payment of contributions, especially in the Gulf, NORKA also provides a form of social security, which allows those returning to receive a pension or some form of allowance in the case of the unemployed or victims of accidents. Remember that Kerala is the Indian state that invested most in welfare and public services after the reorganisation of the borders and independence from the British Empire in 1947. In fact it boasts the highest rate of literacy and also the highest life expectancy. Among other things it is also the first state in the world to have brought a communist party into government with democratic elections in 1956.

For its part the Indian national government has already regulated some procedures for employment abroad through bilateral agreements with the countries of the Middle East and the Gulf, establishing minimum wages and a range of protection. In the last few years the level of debate has increased regarding the need to have a migration policy with international dimensions, because in South East Asia, India is the only country not only of origin, but also of transit and destination for migrant labour. There are many Bangladeshis or Nepalis crossing the border every day who are attracted by the economic development the subcontinent is investing in. Apart from the trade unions, there are various non-government associations and organisations putting pressure on the government so that a new migration policy with an holistic approach will soon be adopted, 'which is based on respect for human rights and ensures security and protection for all migrants, qualified and unqualified, men and women, legal and illegal, leaving and arriving'.[47] For this reason groups connected with the Migrant Forum in Asia (MFA) continue to ask for ratification of the UN Convention on the Rights of All Migrant Workers and Members of Their Families.[48]

In any case the problem with Kerala is no different from that of Nepal, where the majority of migrants move through private recruitment agencies. These have offices throughout the country, even in the remotest areas, in the countryside, where they often take advantage of the ignorance and naivety of the very young.[49] Contracts soon turn out to be swindles, because at the time of the migrants' departure from Kathmandu the middlemen present a new agreement under worse conditions. Anyone already committed, who is often in debt to pay the agency and obtain work, is then forced to accept it. Once the migrant reaches his destination, he discovers that the contract signed in Nepal is not valid in the new country and almost always the terms subsequently become worse, with lower pay and longer hours. Language complicates matters, because agreements are written predominantly in English and few people really understand what they are reading. In 2008 the Nepali trade union federation GEFONT started the 'Safe Migration' campaign in 13 provinces, sending their representatives from village to village to provide information on the safest way to emigrate and to avoid swindles.

"We cannot stop this flow of migrants leaving, because our economy is too weak and we depend on remittances," says the General Secretary of GEFONT, Umesh Upadhyaya. "But we must do what we can to make work safe and to do this we must make any collective demand together with the trade unions and human rights groups of the receiving countries."[50] In fact Nepali unions are also trying to create links with other organisations to accompany their workers. There is a specific agreement with Malaysian wood trade unions, for example, so that registered Nepali workers are followed individually. And in Hong Kong the organisation of construction workers has united locals and migrants in a single structure. In the Gulf also, where this may have seemed almost impossible until a few years ago, in January 2012 the Nepali federation succeeded in signing an agreement with the trade unions of Bahrain and Kuwait to make it easier to move and prevent exploitation by middlemen through guidance and assistance on arrival. The agreement is particularly important for domestic workers, who represent almost half of the 40,000 Nepali migrants in Kuwait, and who are often abused by employers. Without this kind of cooperation and 'in the absence of a solid legal framework and rigorous monitoring activity,' comments Abdulrahman Alghanim, General Secretary of the Kuwaiti federation KTUF, 'recruitment agencies will continue to practise this new form of slave trade.'[51]

The tower of Armani and of Athiraman

'Soaring high above Downtown Dubai in the iconic Burj Khalifa, the world's tallest building, Armani Hotel Dubai, is the world's first hotel designed and developed by Giorgio Armani. Reflecting the pure elegance, simplicity and sophisticated comfort that define Armani's signature style, the hotel is the realisation of the designer's long-held dream to bring his sophisticated style to life in the most complete way and offer his customers a Stay with Armani experience.'[52]

This flowery presentation on the website of the Burj Khalifa describes the hotel occupying several floors of the skyscraper that is the symbol of Dubai, with 108 rooms and 52 suites at an average cost of €700 a night, various public spaces and a spa of more than 12,000 square metres. Coming into the entrance hall, which is in front of the lounge bar, the 'sophisticated comfort' of Armani immediately makes itself felt under the soft lights and high ceilings. The clients are Arab men of the Gulf followed by their families, elderly European and Japanese tourists, and Russian businessmen with girls returning from shopping with large Fendi and Gucci bags. Filipino maids constantly come to tidy up the dark velvet sofas, arranging them very quickly and carefully every time a client gets up. Then they disappear.

Apart from the hotel, the building also boasts the highest swimming pool and mosque in the world. Burj means 'tower' and it was given the name Khalifa as a tribute to the President of the Emirates, Khalifa bin Zayed Al Nahyan. The tower is 828 metres high with 163 floors, and was built in six years at an initial cost of over one and a half billion dollars. In 2008 the property company dealing with sales, Emaar Properties, declared that the price of offices had reached US$43,000 a square metre, and Armani residences were sold at about US$37,500 a square metre.[53]

'Dubai regards this ambitious construction as a metaphor for its role in the vanguard of globalisation as a technocracy capable of combining Islam with modernity,' commented Geraldine Bedell for *The Observer*.[54] The Chicago architects who designed the tower say they were inspired by both the minarets and desert flowers and the ideas of Frank Lloyd Wright, the father of organic architecture. Actually Lloyd Wright often talked about the 'tyranny of skyscrapers' in US cities in the 1930s: 'The success of the vertical is only temporary, in both nature and quality, because the citizens of the near future will prefer the horizontal and will rebel against the vertical, running away from it like the corpse of American cities.'[55]

Instead the highest 'corpse' in the world now rises up in Dubai and is the ideal representation of a model for development based on consumer capitalism, luxury and ostentatious wealth, far from the elegance it aspires to and the sustainability it knows nothing of. In the middle of the desert in a city with the highest level of carbon emissions per capita in the world the air conditioning system of the building alone produces the equivalent of 12,500 tonnes of ice a day. The same logic of environmental irresponsibility has been applied to the Dubailand amusement park, where the Tiger Woods Al Ruwaya golf course requires 18,200 cubic metres of water every day.[56] In Dubai, unsustainability does not stop at natural resources.

The workers who actually built the tower were paid an average of US$200 a month by Arabtec, the largest construction group in the Emirates, for a 12-hour day, six days a week. One of them was Athiraman Kannan, a 38-year-old Indian labourer, who had been in the Gulf for 10 years. In May 2011, before jumping from the 147th floor of the skyscraper, he had told his workmates that he would have to return home to the south of India to resolve a family matter after the death of his brother. But Arabtec refused permission, information that the company was quick to deny immediately after his death. Athiraman was sleeping at the Jebel Ali work camp on the outskirts of Dubai and sending all his money home to support his elderly parents, wife and four-year-old son.[57]

"Every death is shocking to us," declared the Indian ambassador to the Emirates, Lokesh. According to him, the reasons for Athiraman's suicide were principally "depression, financial problems and missing his family". Athiraman's story is not an isolated case. In 2010, 133 Indians killed themselves and in 2008, at the peak of the financial crisis, there were 143 officially recorded deaths. Many were not even reported through fear of the stigma attached to suicide. The embassy started a radio campaign to publicise a service to help workers. The calls showed that most problems were connected with contracts, and not personal matters. In fact, the basic problem remained work. This has also been shown by the many strikes that accompanied the tower's construction. There had been various protest actions to obtain higher wages since March 2006, but Arabtec's management always threatened mass expulsions. The most famous dates back to November 2007, when more than 30,000 migrants downed tools for 10 days. They were asking for an increase of 20 per cent in their wages, which they got in the end but at the cost of many being repatriated.

The economic crisis in the last few years has made the situation worse, because the construction sector has contracted and many migrants are being abandoned by companies closing building sites. Some have been left for months in work camps without money, water or electricity. The last strike at Arabtec was in January 2011, when about 5,000 workers stopped work for two weeks.[58] The demand was for another US$50 dollars a month and the cost of a return journey to their country to be covered. Many also complained about not being paid for overtime. But this time there was no negotiation and 71 Bangladeshis were accused of instigating a revolt in the company camp. They were all arrested and taken away. According to the Dubai police, these were just "people creating disorder", and the ambassador of Bangladesh was of the same opinion: 'The Emirates represent the labour market employing the greatest number of Bangladeshis and the consequences of the illegal actions of some cannot be paid for by all the others.'[59]

Anthropologist Ahmed Kanna has observed the economic and social dynamics of the country for a long time, and maintains that these revolts go beyond the problem relating to wage bargaining: 'They are the result of a combination of various structural elements of the vulnerability of foreigners and elements created by global economic policy and local practises, both in the Emirates and in the countries of origin.'[60] In short, this is a convergence between policies and exploitative practices that occur when leaving and arriving on the migration route, in the new international division of labour. Migrants are kept without rights in their countries of destination and are left to fend for themselves by their own governments, being exploited by middlemen and traffickers. This is a multiple attack, therefore, which according to Kanna brings out the complete contradiction of this system and all its potential for conflict: 'Even though they are excluded and exploited, the migrants in the Gulf are far from being the passive, silent slaves we tend to imagine.'

Like everybody else, like nobody else

In the long chain of migrant work, particularly in the countries of the Middle East, the Gulf and Asia, the weakest link is domestic servants, particularly when they are women. Although there is little legal protection for work in factories, on building sites or in hotels, domestic work is not even considered a legal matter but a private question, for which only the employing families are responsible. There are no trade unions for domestic work, no national contracts, minimum wages or common parameters. There is even discrimination in remuneration according to gender and nationality, which takes no account of merits and skills. In Malaysia, for example, Filipino domestic servants receive higher salaries than Indonesians, while in Jordan they are better paid than Sri Lankans and Ethiopians.[61]

These migrants must therefore rely on the protection measures introduced by the governments in the countries of origin that are often the result of bilateral agreements or intervention by embassies. The Filipino government has arranged reception centres in the major cities of the Gulf, the Middle East and Asia for cases of mistreatment as described earlier, in order to accommodate women who are the victims of violence and trafficking. According to information from the Visayan Forum Foundation NGO, there was a 20 per cent increase in the trafficking of people in the Philippines between 2008 and 2009. Cecilia Flores Oebanda, President of the Foundation, points out that there are a million domestic servants 'exported' but almost double this number work in the Philippines and their conditions are certainly not better: 'First we must think of putting things in order ourselves, if we want others also to respect our workers.'[62] For now the government has imposed a series of requirements for domestic servants who emigrate, such as a minimum age of 18, a basic wage of US$400 dollars a month, attending guidance courses and public recruitment agencies being banned from asking for money from migrants. It is striking that those taking advantage of migrants are not only traffickers or employers, but also sometimes the officials of their own national institutions.

The Migrante International association has been dealing with the protection of Filipinos abroad since 1996. It was created after a domestic servant, unjustly accused of homicide, was sentenced to death in Singapore. Today it works in 22 countries and pursues disputes and campaigns, including against the government of Manila, criticised for 'the policy of exporting and commercialising national workers'.[63] Nhel Morona is the General Secretary of Migrante in the United Arab Emirates, where more than 400,000 Filipinos live, and in 2011, together with other organisations, launched a petition to remove a bureaucratic practice that makes blackmail and extortion easier. In 2010 various immigration officials were accused of extorting money from the family members of migrants visiting the Emirates.

In fact, in order to leave, a series of documents was required and authorisation had to be issued by local authorities, in addition to the entry visa for a temporary visit.[64] Several travellers reported that some public officials were claiming money – from €250 to €500 per person – just before leaving Ninoy Aquino International Airport. The Interministerial Council against Trafficking imposed more transparent and more secure procedures on the Immigration Office, even though, in order to prevent any risk, 'the current system of selection would need to be removed completely,' commented Morona.[65]

This case confirms what was indicated by Ahmed Kanna regarding the 'combination of various structural elements in the vulnerability of foreigners'[66] in both the countries of destination and those of origin, where corrupt officials may speculate on the poorest of their fellow countrymen. Therefore migrants are faced with a double attack, on both departing and arriving, and in the case of domestic work those protecting it are essentially human rights associations and activists. Visayan and Migrante certainly represent good examples of *advocacy* but nevertheless these are organisations reserved for national workers, which in fact exclude any other potential people to be protected, if they are not Filipino. The scope of protection may only really be widened through transnational networks made up of associations and trade unions, like those developed between India and Bahrain or between Nepal and Malaysia.

Meanwhile, it is good that domestic work is becoming subject to regulation, including in some countries in the Middle Eastern region. In Lebanon in 2009 the Department of Employment set up an appropriate national contract with clearer standards. The main elements were the working day lasting a maximum of 10 hours and employers being obliged to pay for one day of rest per week, annual paid holiday and sick leave on a monthly basis through a bank transfer. However, domestic servants could not leave a job without the written permission of the person who had taken them on.[67] Before Lebanon, it was Jordan that adopted some specific standards for domestic servants in 2003 and introduced domestic work into its legislation between 2008 and 2009. According to a report by Human Rights Watch in 2011, however, actual conditions have not changed, and more than 70,000 Filipino, Sri Lankan and Indonesian domestic servants are suffering the same abuse as in other countries in the region.[68]

What might make a difference today, in terms of regulations, is the International Convention on Domestic Workers, adopted by the International Conference on Labour in Geneva on 16 June 2011. Associations, NGOs and trade unions are all putting pressure on governments to ratify the new ILO Convention, No 189, in order to ensure protection and respect for fundamental rights in the countries of destination (see below).[69] The regulations will especially establish that domestic servants have the same rights as are recognised for other workers: reasonable hours, a weekly rest of at least 24 consecutive hours, a limit to payment in kind and clear information on the terms and conditions of employment as well as respect for basic principles, freedom of association and the right to collective bargaining. The ILO estimates that there are at least 53 million home helps and carers in the world, although the figure is certainly higher, since many are not registered. For developing countries they represent up to 12 per cent of salaried workers and are largely migrant women.

The result of the adoption of a specific convention that is binding for the government that ratifies it is even more significant when you consider that domestic servants do not represent a strong professional category linked to a defined economic sector with a tradition of trade union representation. In fact, according to the slogan of a recent campaign, domestic servants 'Work like everybody else, work like nobody else.'

Notwithstanding these limits, the text was voted for by more than two thirds of the delegates present at the ILO conference, representing the governments, employers and trade unions of the 183 member states of the ILO. The General Secretary of the ITUC, Sharan Burrow,[70] asked the ILO to put pressure on governments to ratify it. According to Burrow, without adequate protection domestic servants will continue to live in inhuman and repressive working conditions, to which must be added the abuse perpetrated by recruitment agencies.

At the end of 2011, the ITUC and other international organisations[71] launched the '12 by 12 campaign' in 81 countries to get at least 12 ratifications by the end of 2012 and to strengthen domestic workers' unions. The government of Uruguay was the first to ratify Convention No 189 in April 2012 and the Philippines, which is a major world supplier of domestic labour, followed in August. Other governments are expected to follow soon, including South Africa, Mauritius, Belgium, Kenya, Brazil and Colombia.[72]

2

In the United States

Hermanos en el camino

The Mexican media called it 'the biggest massacre of recent years'. The 72 migrants the police found inside an old ranch in San Fernando in north-east Mexico on 25 August 2010 came from Brazil, Ecuador, El Salvador and Honduras and were trying to cross the border into the US. There were 58 men and 14 women and they were all piled up in an abandoned warehouse against the wall, one on top of the other, face down, their hands tied behind their backs and their eyes blindfolded. A real execution. Not even a cloth to cover the bodies.

The CNN news story is still on YouTube with journalists reconstructing the dynamics of the events and showing maps with the exact point where the slaughter took place, just 160 kilometres from Brownsville in Texas. As if to say they had almost made it. A few metres from the border they ran into the Zetas gang, which controls drug trafficking in the territory and also profits from immigration. Criminal groups usually abduct migrants and demand a ransom from their families in the US, up to US$3,000 per person, or enlist them in trade and trafficking. This time, however, it seems the 72 had refused either to pay or to work for the traffickers. The only one who escaped, a boy from Ecuador, managed to get out of the warehouse and reached the nearest US roadblock. The marines immediately sent helicopters to the ranch and started a shoot-out with the Zetas men. One soldier and two traffickers died before they burst into the ranch where they found an arsenal, and some members of the gang were arrested.

The Mexican government spokesman for security, Alejandro Poire, declared: 'It is a terrible act and demands condemnation by the whole of our society.'[1] But associations defending human rights rose up, demanding more than simple declarations and accusing the executive of the former conservative President of Mexico, Felipe Calderón, of inertia. Calderón, who was elected in 2006, had made the fight against drug trafficking his slogan. "Mexico bears great responsibility for the constant violation of the human rights of migrants, these are crimes against humanity which may not be considered simple actions by criminal gangs," maintains Elvira Arellano, leader of the Movimento Mesoamericano de Migrantes.[2] Amnesty International also talked of a 'human rights crisis' in 2010 and called crossing Mexico 'one of the most dangerous journeys in the world.'[3] Formal protests to the Mexican Ministry for Foreign Affairs also came from the governments of Guatemala, El Salvador and Honduras, because of the incompetence of the authorities in the face of violence against their citizens; they demanded that at the very least an inquiry be set up into the kidnappings and the killings. Like the poorest countries in South East Asia, work by migrants also fuels the national economy in Central America, however. Remittances make up 176 per cent of GDP in Honduras, 165 per cent in Ecuador and 108 per cent in Guatemala.[4] According to the National Commission for Human Rights, working in Mexico in a civil defence capacity, kidnappings of migrants were happening at a rate of 1,600 people a month between 2008 and 2009. The latest information available from the Office of the Mexican Attorney-General, for the period from 2006 to 2012, talks of over 47,500 victims of the drug-related human trafficking and violence.[5]

In order to provide assistance and prevent trafficking, in 2007 the Hermanos en el Camino protection centre was set up in the State of Oaxaca, the poorest region of the country, as well as in Chiapas and Guerrero. Its founder, Father José Alejandro Solalinde Guerra, chose as its headquarters the small town of Ixtepec, the point of convergence between the Pacific Ocean, the Gulf of Mexico and flows of migrants coming from the south; Guatemala, in fact, is only 350 kilometres away. "The majority of migrants travel on top of goods trains and during the journey, which lasts for days, many are attacked and the women are also raped. They suffer extortion by the municipal, state and federal police as well as the immigration agency," recount activists at the centre.[6] For some time Father Solalinde denounced connivance by the police with the traffickers and received several death threats because of this, until, under pressure from the

Inter-American Commission for Human Rights, the government had to supply an escort for him.

The National Institute for Immigration (Instituto Nacional de Migración, INM), responsible for repatriating illegal migrants, has been subject to an inquiry because of alleged corruption and possible offences during kidnapping operations. According to reports by the Department of Public Prosecution of Oaxaca, Father Solalinde declared that these attacks were due to corruption and complicity by the state authorities with organised crime, and that traffickers had approached him to work with them rather than try to rescue migrants. As in the countries of the Gulf, the UN Commissioner for Human Rights, Navi Pillay, also intervened. After the umpteenth case of extortion and kidnapping – this time of 40 people on board a train near Oaxaca, including 10 women and a child, in January 2011 – the Commissioner publicly demanded 'an extensive and transparent inquiry into the alleged mistreatment and abuse of migrants by the Federal Police and staff of the INM'.[7] The agency received so many reports of the violation of human rights that in April 2011 the government dismissed seven top executives, suspected of collusion with criminals. In May Calderón wanted a new law on immigration that would protect those crossing the country better and punish officials involved in cases of corruption more severely. The government was given credit for this measure by several parties, but in view of the distance there is in Mexico between a text and its application, the law alone does not seem enough to improve and reduce the dangers.[8]

The new Mexican President, Enrique Peña Nieto, called for renewed debate on the 'drug war' but said that the government should focus more on reducing violence and less on catching cartel leaders or stopping drugs from reaching the United States. Peña Nieto, of the Institutional Revolutionary Party, PRI, was elected in mid-2012 amid accusations of vote-buying.[9] Running into drug cartels is not the only risk to be found on the border between Mexico and the United States. The US journalist Margaret Regan has collected harrowing stories of those trying to cross the desert to the North West on the border with Arizona.[10] There migrants place their trust in the *coyote*, traffickers, who have no hesitation in abandoning them at the first sign of border police or if one of the travellers cannot keep going. In 2008 this happened to Josseline Jasimeth Hernández, 14 years old, from El Salvador, who was with her younger brother on the way to join their mother, Sonia, in Los Angeles. The children had stayed with relatives until Sonia had put away enough money for them to leave as well. The journey had been hard – 2,000 kilometres across El Salvador, Guatemala and the south of Mexico. The group had travelled by bus and train, crossed mountains and rivers and stopped wherever they happened to be. In the end, however, they succeeded in leaving Mexico behind and reaching Arizona in the Sonor Desert. The difference in temperature there between day and night is great, and January is right in the middle of the rainy season. After the last stop, before going back to the car to finally enter the US, Josseline started to get stomach ache, with severe attacks of vomiting.

The girl had no strength and the group could not wait. So the *coyote* decided to leave her there, in the middle of nowhere, among the cacti and the reptiles, in the rain and the freezing night. According to a trafficker this was an area patrolled by the border police, the *migra*, as the Mexicans call it, with cars and helicopters, so they believed that she would soon be found. When her brother arrived in Los Angeles some days later, her mother called the Salvadoran consulate in Nogales, a small town on the border. Activists from Coalición de Derechos Umanos and No More Deaths, humanitarian organisations that try to track down the missing, were also mobilised. After three weeks of searching, Josseline's body was found a few hundred metres from the point where she had been left. She was leaning on a rock with her hands by her head, as though to protect herself from the cold. They recognised her by her clothes, but in view of the climatic conditions the state of decomposition was such that it was necessary to carry out a DNA test in order to establish her identity.

In the early years of the 1990s cases of migrants who died or went missing in the Arizona desert, along a border 606 kilometres long, could be counted on the fingers of one hand, but the figure since then has started to rise rapidly. Bruce Parks is the police doctor for the county of Pima and the first to confirm the deaths, which are due mainly to exposure or dehydration, but also drowning in the case of those trying to cross the rivers, or road accidents. According to Parks' accounts there may have been more than 1,700 deaths in 10 years.[11] Margaret Regan attributes the responsibility for so many tragedies to the policies of militarising the borders started by the Clinton administration, which wanted to respond to the immigration alarm given by the Republicans and therefore attempt to reduce the presence of illegal immigrants, particularly in the towns of California and Arizona.[12] The first significant control operations, Hold the Line in Texas and Operation Gatekeeper in California, were in 1993 and 1994. A hard line was used to stop illegal immigration once and for all, with the harsh nature of the desert the principal deterrent. But the politicians were wrong, and the victims of the desert soon increased. 'Deaths from crossing the border have doubled since 1995,' the report by the Government Accountability Office submitted to the US Senate in 2006 stated in no uncertain terms.[13] The situation has become worse since 9/11. The agency for immigration and naturalisation has become part of the Department of Homeland Security, which was famously created by George W. Bush, and the border police have started to treat every migrant as a potential terrorist.

The work borderline

Mexico is in a special situation, because it is a country of both transit and origin. In fact there are even more Mexicans trying to cross the border with the United States than Guatemalans, Salvadorans, Hondurans and Latin Americans. The US economy has always benefited from the low-cost manpower coming from its first neighbour to the South, but the economic reforms of the 1990s increased the rate and intensity of flows without improving working conditions. The journalist David Bacon[14] dates the start of this phase back to 1994, to the speculative attack on Mexican debt by US banks following the North American Free Trade Agreement (NAFTA) coming into force. NAFTA was aimed at making trade between Canada, the US and Mexico easier by doing away with customs and export tariffs, but it soon proved to be just a way of allowing the US market to expand.

The Mexican agricultural market was opened to heavily subsidised US producers, and this caused the bankruptcy of many small farmers. In the border area, where most of the factories (the *maquiladoras*) are located, "government restrictions on trade union freedom and the high rate of unemployment contributed to bringing down wages,"[15] explains Javier Rodriguez, a political activist and trade unionist. The result is that more and more people have started to emigrate to the north and the number of illegal immigrants has more than doubled, from less than 5 million in 1994 to more than 12 million in 2007, about half from Mexico and a quarter from Central and Latin America. All this took place while Washington was reducing the number of temporary visas and sealing the border to the south.

According to the latest report by the Labour Council for Latin American Advancement (LCLAA), after almost 20 years NAFTA has only contributed to making the conditions of both the Central American and the US working class worse. Wages have gone down and the gap between rich and poor has widened.[16] In Mexico about 30 million people survive on less than 30 pesos (little more than US$2 dollars) a day and almost 40 per cent of the population are living below the poverty line. So it comes as no surprise to know that currently Mexicans represent 21 per cent of legal migrants and 59 per cent of illegal migrants in the US.[17] Many prefer to leave Mexico, even at the cost of going through traffickers and at the cost of living as an 'illegal alien'.

There are two types of temporary visa Latin American migrants may hope to obtain as non-specialist workers or as guest workers. Both are used to fill positions for which a temporary lack of national manpower has been recognised.[18] The first, H-2A, has a maximum duration of one year, it may be renewed for up to three and is used in particular for agricultural work during harvests or for other short-term jobs on farms. When employers make a request for this visa, they have to then offer full-time employment with a contract and clear information on terms of payment and conditions, also undertaking to cover the incidental costs of transport and accommodation. Work allowed with H-2A visas, currently about 30,000 in circulation, is equivalent to US work and therefore in theory provides the same protection and wage levels. For the other type of permit, H-2B, there is a limit to entries every year – about 66,000 in 2011 – but there are no special professional requirements and there is no equivalence with the conditions of national contracts, let alone a minimum number of hours to be guaranteed. There is only a vague reference to the obligation to make wages fall in line with the best conditions offered in the area.[19]

Given that a large proportion of travelling expenses are charged to the migrants, the system also allows companies to request an unnecessary number of workers for agriculture, forestry work, the food industry, construction and other sectors in need of manpower with low qualifications. This excess availability and lack of control in some sectors obviously creates distortions in the labour market, fuels illegality and subsequently allows costs to be brought down. Many stay after their visa has expired in order to at least repay the debt they have accrued, and therefore swell the ranks of the many undocumented already living in the most insecure situations.

The Southern Poverty Law Center (SPLC), an Alabama group defending human rights, published a report denouncing the complete ineffectiveness of the H2 programme and showing how this mechanism encouraged work on the black market, abuse and mistreatment.[20] Unlike US citizens, foreigners do not enjoy the most basic freedom and protection of a truly competitive labour market, much less the possibility of changing employment if they are exploited. SPLC activists maintain that guest workers are completely bound to the employer who 'imports' them, and if they try to complain or even make a report, as provided by the law, they are immediately put on blacklists or deported. The little protection envisaged by the Department of Employment for H-2A visas 'remains on paper', and no private lawyer would ever undertake to defend the rights of migrants. Therefore they become easy victims of abuse. They are constantly swindled out of wages and pay very high interest – up to 20 per cent – on the debts they contract with recruitment agencies before their departure and are not able to honour in view of the discontinuous nature of the work and low pay. Furthermore, they are often forced to live in a situation of constant blackmail and virtual slavery because of their dependence on their employer, who has no hesitation in withholding their social security cards and passports.[21]

It cannot fail to be noted that this is essentially the same dependency already seen in the countries of the Persian Gulf where the system of sponsorship, *kafala*, is in force and it is private individuals and companies, not the states, who make decisions on the migrant labour market. 'There is an imbalance of power between employer and worker, which is completely in favour of the former,' clarifies the report by the SPLC, 'to the point where the rights of immigrants end up being wiped out. The employer may sack the seasonal worker, call the authorities and report him as illegal at any time.' The story of Juan, a Guatemalan labourer, is indicative: "The boss took away our passports as soon as we arrived from Mexico and wouldn't hear a word about giving them back to us. Even when he paid us by cheque and we needed our passports to change the money into cash, there was nothing we could do, he kept telling us those were the rules. But if my passport lets me be here legally without any problem, what do I do to show I'm not illegal?"[22] According to a report by Human Rights Watch on the application of the H-2A system in North Carolina, blackmail and fear are extremely widespread among legal migrants, and there is proof of blacklists against those who dare to question working conditions, seek legal assistance or attempt trade union organisation.[23]

The situation is no better regarding working conditions. According to SPLC, wages are rarely in line with the national minimum levels provided and companies sometimes pay per unit of product. Those working in reforestation, for example, are paid based on the number of plants sown in 12-hour shifts, six days a week, with payment ranging from US$22.50 to US$45 a day, way below minimum levels. In many cases the responsibility for these violations is lost in the supplier chain. In 2006 in South Georgia SPLC began a class action against the Del Monte Group, representing some Mexican labourers who had been underpaid. Whole families had moved from Mexico, attracted by promises of working for a major brand like Del Monte, but it had then been middlemen with no actual agricultural business who had drawn up the documents and dictated the conditions.[24]

To the question of wages must be added that of logistics, which in this case also does not seem to differ much from the segregation practised in the countries of the Gulf. In the agricultural sector companies often provide squalid accommodation, prefabs and containers on the extreme outskirts of urban centres or in the open countryside, in many cases without services such as telephone and transport, and without electricity.[25] At this point dependency on employers is total. Another worrying fact about guest workers concerns health and safety risks. Workers with temporary contracts meet with accidents more easily, and have more difficulty getting insurance or obtaining healthcare. The figures speak for themselves: from 1992 to 2007 the number of fatal accidents among Latin Americans increased by 76 per cent and the number of Central and South Americans dying on the job – equal to 937 – exceeded the national average by 21 per cent.[26] Of these, more than 600 were immigrants, employed predominantly in the building industry in the states of Texas, Florida and California, where the concentration of undocumented immigrants is very high.

A nation of immigrants

One of John Fitzgerald Kennedy's most famous works, *A nation of immigrants*, opened with verses by the American poet Walt Whitman: 'These States are the greatest poetry, here there is not only a nation but a fertile Nation of nations.' The message Kennedy wanted to give about his idea of society at that time was clear: 'Everywhere immigrants have enriched and reinforced the fabric of life in the United States and, if the country is really to be known, this particular American revolution needs to be understood.'[27] The book contained an accurate analysis of the history of immigration and some political proposals for new admission criteria to regulate entry quotas according to the principles of equality, justice and humanity.

Together with Canada and Australia, the United States is the English-speaking nation most built on mass migration from a cultural, social and economic point of view. The American people are still aware of this today. The concept of territory remains the key to membership and citizenship, rather than origin or descent, as happens instead in the European tradition. Since the 1868 Constitution, obtaining the right to citizenship was established by *jus soli*, the fact of being born in the territory, just like residence in the country today may give the right to naturalisation under certain conditions. Beyond the legal question, the political culture of the US itself was based on the 18th-century idea of the 'new man' as a result of the mixture of people and cultures with different origins.[28] Nevertheless, on the subject of admission and integration of new Americans there is no doubt that the dominant WASP (White Anglo-Saxon Protestant) component developed a policy of assimilation towards the millions of immigrants reaching and populating the country with the exclusion of indigenous people and forced African immigrants.

The first law on citizenship in 1790 established that 'free white immigrants' who had been resident for at least two years were entitled to this right, denying the possibility of obtaining it to Africans, Asians, temporary workers and the majority of women.[29] The restrictions were such that in 1882 Congress approved the 'law excluding the Chinese' in order to limit their entry for reasons that were partly protectionist and partly cultural, because they were thought to be too distant from European origin and therefore difficult to assimilate. The way Chinese families were hunted was brutal, so much so that the scholar Jean Pfaelzer has written of a 'forgotten war' against Chinese Americans.[30]

In spite of this, US rhetoric continued to be built around the idea of the 'crucible of races wanted by God', represented by the expression *melting pot*, conceived by the English comedy writer of Jewish origin, Israel Zangwill, who had idealised the fusion of different people into a new identity with new opportunities.[31] The growth in flows of migrants has been maintained since 1820, particularly from Ireland, Great Britain, Germany and France. The civil wars in the 1840s to 1850s throughout Europe and the famine in Ireland in 1845 represented some of the main expulsion factors. But growing industrialisation and the discovery of large gold deposits in California also constituted attraction factors for people from Asia and Mexico. In spite of new restrictions and the imposition of quotas, such as in 1924,[32] immigration continued to grow quickly, also including workers and families from southern Europe – Italy, Spain and Greece – until the economic crisis in 1929.

The Great Depression led the government to carry out a vast repatriation plan, and until the Second World War entry possibilities were drastically reduced, being limited to Europeans. As a result of having taken part in the conflict, this brought out the need for a labour force in agriculture, and from 1942 to 1964 the Bracero ['Farm worker'] Program was adopted to attract Mexican workers and peasants, but for a fixed time.[33] After the Second World War immigration resumed in changing phases, also because of sizeable flows of European and Jewish refugees as well as Russians, Poles and Hungarians from the countries of the Soviet block. In 1965 the quota system for countries of origin was replaced by quotas for reunions through the family 'sponsor', granting entry to those who already had a relative who was a US citizen, and quotas for work reasons, for workers recruited by a company. The new criteria were also based on the promotion of diversification by hemisphere with limits of about 120,000 entries a year for the West (the American continent) and 170,000 for the East. Limits were not set on temporary specialist workers or asylum-seekers. Admission and inclusion policies followed a multicultural approach, living together based on respect for diversity, according to those values of equality referred to by J.F. Kennedy and to the principle of the *salad bowl*. This term indicated a single society made up of ingredients that were different, but did not blend, unlike the *melting pot*.

From the open multiculturalism of the 1970s, however, many Americans moved on to widespread hostility towards migrants. Flows also changed, with a large reduction in Western Europeans and a constant increase in workers from Mexico, Central Southern America and Asia. Throughout the 1970s pro-immigrant activists protested against a series of bills aimed at repressing or criminalising foreigners. A wave of demonstrations in 1984 and pressure on the Latin American component of the establishment persuaded the Democrats to amend the law, which was then under discussion, until the approval of a real reform. In 1986 the US adopted the Immigration Reform and Control Act (IRCA), which is still in force today, and introduced a series of measures to reduce illegal entries with more severe penalties for those using workers without documents. At the same time an amnesty for agriculture led to 2,700,000 people having their status regularised. The 1986 reform also set up a commission to study the reasons for economic migration to the US. Based on the results of this research it was felt necessary to create a free trade area in the North American region to regulate and manage flows better, which is how NAFTA came to be drawn up in 1994.[34]

In the early years of the 1990s xenophobic tendencies also increased because of the rhetoric of some Republican exponents, chief among them the ex-television journalist Pat Buchanan. 'This was our land and nobody else's,' wrote Buchanan in one of his books, 'but today America and Great Britain have espoused the idea of the natural equality of all cultures, civilisations and languages and the mixture of all tribes, races and peoples. Not only is this antihistoric, but it is suicide for America and the West.'[35] It is not by chance that in those years the Democratic administration of Bill Clinton restricted the number of legal entries and started the first projects for militarising the border between Mexico and the US. The terrorist attacks in 2001 subsequently made the situation worse, fuelling xenophobia towards some groups, particularly Arabs and Muslims.

In the early years of the 2000s many anti-immigrant groups were also formed, such as Save our State (SOS) in California, which went into working offices to intimidate foreigners, and the Minutemen Vigilantes of Jim Gilchrist, an ex-marine. "They took the name from an extreme right group, which used to attack militants of the movement against the war in Vietnam in the 60s," recounts Javier Rodriguez.[36] In 2005 the Minutemen organised expeditions to patrol the border between Arizona and Mexico, hunting for migrants without documents to be reported, and Arnold Schwarzenegger, former governor of California, publicly praised these initiatives. According to information from LCLAA, attacks against Latin American migrants increased by 40 per cent in the US from 2003 to 2007. Central and Latin Americans also represent 62 per cent of the victims of crimes linked to nationality and 'race'.[37]

Faced with the question of illegal immigrants in the US, about 12 million in 2004, the Bush administration proposed a first action for reform through an amnesty for three million people and a programme to link permits more to work than reunions according to the temporary guest worker model. Through the amnesty the Republicans hoped to obtain approval from among the Latino component, a strongly growing part of the American population. But the initial proposal ran aground in the first debates. In December 2005 the Republican majority in the House of Representatives decided to adopt another approach, approving a particularly rigid bill. The Border Protection, Antiterrorism and Illegal Immigration Control Act, HR 4437,[38] had been presented by the Republican deputy for Wisconsin, James Sensenbrenner, who wanted to make immigration without documents an offence. The proposed law would punish anyone offering work to illegal migrants and authorise the construction of a barrier between the US and Mexico stretching more than 1,000 kilometres.

The Great American Boycott

After approval by the House of Representatives of the Sensenbrenner Bill, which associated guarding the borders with anti-terrorism measures, various groups and networks of immigrants of Hispanic origin, together with US human rights activists, started to plan actions demonstrating against the reform passing to the Senate.

A grassroots information and opposition campaign soon developed within various communities of immigrants through television and radio stations and websites, but also parish churches and trade unions, involving some well-known media people, such as Eduardo Sotelo, the key radio presenter for the Latin American community.[39] On 14 February 2006 in Philadelphia, Pennsylvania, migrant workers from various restaurants in the city called a spontaneous 24-hour strike, demonstrating symbolically in the square where the Declaration of Independence was signed in 1776. In spite of the small number of demonstrators, about 2,000 people, the action attracted media attention to the reasons for the protest, which had the effect of increasing strikes, boycotts and marches in the following weeks from Chicago to Milwaukee, with growing numbers taking part.

Los Angeles pro-immigrant groups called the first significant demonstration on 25 March, when support exceeded all expectations, reaching 500,000 people. Although entirely peaceful without any clashes, the Grande Marcha, as it was called, stopped traffic in the city centre for hours. At that point the protests had reached across the whole country from coast to coast and from north to south.

The organisers of the individual groups quickly became coordinated in a new network, the May Day Movement for Workers' and Immigrants' Rights, which at the end of April already had an official membership of 200 different organisations, from Afro-American to Chinese communities, to call a national day of protest and boycott on 1 May.[40] There is an 'irony of history' when you think that this date is a workers' holiday throughout the world except in the US, although it actually started in the US. There were the famous clashes in Haymarket Square in Chicago on 1 May 1886, where thousands of workers, predominantly European immigrants, demonstrated to get an eight-hour day. There were several deaths as a result of the provocation and repression by the police, and four activists, who were accused of inciting the crowd, were hanged. They were all trade unionists and thought to be anarchists.[41] The commemoration of 1 May was taken off the calendar in the US in the anti-communist climate of the Cold War, when Socialist International chose it as the key date for the labour movement.

Instead, the 2006 movement used the networks of migration chains, social networks and Spanish language media to spread its message online: documented and undocumented immigrants were to take part in demonstrations against the HR 4437 reform, stopping work, shopping and school, but in a peaceful, even 'patriotic' way. In fact the demonstrators were to wave the US flag alongside that of their country of origin as a mark of gratitude to the land and people hosting them. The choice of the slogan 'A day without immigrants' contributed to the media success of the mobilisation. The expression paraphrased and extended the concept expressed in the 2004 comedy film, *A day without a Mexican*, by Sergio Arau,[42] in which the sudden disappearance of all Mexican workers from California was portrayed, leaving companies, offices, schools and families in chaos. The slogan also indicated the way the protest would take shape, in the form of a day of economic boycott through a strike on working and spending, that is to say, in the dual economic role of migrants as workers and consumers. Reactions to the announcement of the strike day came immediately from several parties: from more moderate pro-immigrant groups, frightened by the negative impact the initiative would have on its citizens, to Republican politicians, who asked them to find other forms of dissent, and including bishops, who offered to take part in commemorative masses for the migrants who had died on the border.

There was no lack of confusion, even within the movement, which feared repercussions and retaliations against workers after the strike. The Service Employees International Union (SEIU), various NGOs, associations of foreigners, the Catholic Church and some politicians of the Democratic Party set up an alternative group, the We are America coalition, and wanted to move the demonstration to the evening so as to avoid striking during the day. While the activists of the Grande Marcha were asking for an unconditional amnesty for the 12 million undocumented, those of the We are America coalition were also in favour of making it easier to obtain citizenship. In the end it was decided to create a wider coalition with different demonstrations for 1 May, which would include the Great American Boycott 'A day without immigrants'. Demands were summed up in 10 points. The first concerned the amnesty for all immigrants without documents, then there was 'No to the barrier along the border', 'No to the criminalisation of illegal immigrants' and 'Stop the round-ups and deportations breaking up families'.[43]

The support of the AFL-CIO (American Federation of Labor and Congress of Industrial Organizations) trade union central body, which was already opposed to the Sensenbrenner Bill, contributed to motivating and reassuring the organisers. The local headquarters and individual branches also had a decisive role in managing the demonstration.[44] In Los Angeles the unions provided volunteers and transport, also collecting the US$80,000 used to prepare for the march. The National Immigrant Solidarity Network (NISN) was put in charge of coordination via the internet, with the creation of networks, mailing lists and contacts.

On 1 May 2006 more than 1.5 million people took to the streets in 70 different cities, even though most marches were held in the centres most populated by immigrants: 250,000 in New York, more than 500,000 in Chicago and 700,000 in Los Angeles. The economic impact of the boycott is more difficult to estimate, particularly in small companies, even though some sectors were literally stopped. Javier Rodriguez was among the organisers of the protest and tells how in Los Angeles alone 75 per cent of companies employing immigrants came to a halt, and 90 per cent of lorry drivers working in ports went on strike.[45] In the fields of California and Arizona fruit and vegetables remained on plants, and the food industries, where most of the workers are foreigners, had to stop production. At Tyson Foods and Cargill Meat Solutions they closed three factories, while Goya Foods, the largest Hispanic distribution chain, suspended deliveries as a mark of solidarity. In many cases these employers demonstrated together with their employees, and in schools and universities, students who were the children of immigrants did not go to class. 'It was more than a reaction to a law by the Congress, it was the response to years of attack and denigration aimed at immigrants and minorities,' comments David Bacon.[46] In fact the most important result was political. The protests succeeded in introducing substantial modifications to the Bill, which at that point came to a halt in the Senate because of its obvious divergence from the text approved by the House, and it was completely abandoned in the end.

Intolerable for a democracy

The other result of the Great American Boycott in 2006 is that it demonstrated the capacity for reaction and resistance in the face of an institutional attack such as the reform by the Bush administration. It demonstrated how strong social networks developed by immigrants could be, both spontaneously and working within associations and large labour organisations. The attitude of US trade unions is changing compared with the closed protectionism of the past, also because a large proportion of new members is made up of immigrants who are reactivating and revitalising old structures. It must be remembered that the US trade union movement is made up of many independent organisations gathered together in two large central bodies, the AFL-CIO, formed in the 1950s, and the most recent coalition, Change to Win. There is therefore a tendency towards a high degree of fragmentation and a relatively low level of representation compared with other industrialised countries such as in Europe. Today in the US, about 12 out of 100 active workers are trade unionised, whereas in the 1950s the membership was close to half.[47]

Indeed, as far as the relationship between trade unions and immigrants is concerned, the political analyst Immanuel Ness maintains that foreigners are more inclined to organise and make demands than locals.[48] US workers of European origin, like those of other developed countries, seem to be suffering from growing individualism, which is dominating the socioeconomic sphere and also pervading the trade union area. Immigrants, who are mostly Hispanic and Asian, instead tend to bring their collectivist traditions with them, which are built around the family and community and then developed within migration networks and social networks, as shown by the example of the demonstrations in Los Angeles. The latest report by the Center for Economic and Policy Research[49] shows that migrants make up 15 per cent of the US workforce and 13 per cent of the trade-unionised workforce. Migrants who are members and more protected than the others are predominantly young men employed full time in manufacturing industry and the private sector. The five largest communities of foreigners are concentrated in California, New York, Texas, Florida and New Jersey, with about a million people in each state. Belonging to a trade union undoubtedly brings advantages: the wages of protected workers are on average 17 per cent higher than those of non-unionised workers, just as their basic hourly pay is about US$2 higher and there are better forms of insurance and social security contributions.[50]

That migrants reinforce the trade union movement and make demands is also shown by another movement that has appeared recently, Justice for Janitors (JFJ),[51] formed predominantly by cleaning workers, home helps and care workers. The creation of JFJ dates back to the mid-1980s as a protest group in the US and Canada against low wages and lack of social security and health protection, made up mostly of Central and Latin American immigrants. Campaigns and strikes were organised by the SEIU, which has almost two million members and also helps foreign communities through training activities to make integration easier. JFJ gained maximum visibility and some famous trade union victories between 2000 and 2006 with a series of protest actions from Los Angeles to Houston and Miami. An excellent portrayal of the fight by cleaners in Los Angeles was given by the English director Ken Loach in the film *Bread and roses*,[52] which shows the abuse, but also the capacity for reaction by migrants in spite of them being at an obvious disadvantage and open to blackmail. The role of the local trade union is decisive, even though not without contradictions, when faced with the difficulty of representing workers with little bargaining power in small companies.

In the case of the 'A day without immigrants' movement in 2006 it was the smallest groups of immigrants and activists who started the protest, using their own channels and social networks independently without the help of traditional representative institutions, specifically trade union central bodies. On a second occasion, when the action had started and shown its potential for agreement, also due to the media impact, these institutions decided to join in and seize the opportunities, providing decisive help. According to Ness, consolidated representative organisations today should offer resources and support for action by migrants, even when this arises from local conflicts in small companies and develops in the informal economy, a dimension traditionally ignored by the unions.[53] However, it is important to respect the independence of these groups that are incorporated and coordinated in wider networks, maybe also made up of other minority groups often discriminated against, such as African-American workers. Research carried out by Ness shows that in the US the best results in terms of working conditions (and not membership and trade union cards) are achieved when this interaction between trade unions and independent groups succeeds in being established. 'Conflicts arising from working relationships in the neoliberal era of globalisation do not necessarily lead to relationships between the trade union and the company in traditional forms,' says Ness.[54]

In the last few years some US trade unions have also developed new strategies of cooperation with workers' organisations in southern countries, in order to try and level the playing field of labour rights and conditions. 'Faced with a choice of reducing our wages or bringing up overseas wages, it is in our interest to do the latter,' says Ben Davis, Director of International Affairs for the United Steelworkers (USW).[55] The idea is to improve farm, factory and shop conditions in Central and Latin America in order to stop job migration to countries with the most abusive sweatshops. USW has helped Mexican mineworkers organise independent affiliates. Those mineworkers, in turn, have held work stoppages in solidarity with USW strikes north of the border.

As for migrants in the US, LCLAA activists lay particular stress on the relationship between unions and illegal immigration.[56] Today the AFL-CIO is active in the area of regularising the status of the undocumented, and the instrumental use the economy is making of them. In the material disseminated through its website the trade union central body explains how social dumping occurs, how the illegality of foreign workers, who are often employed in the same sectors and companies as legal migrants and Americans, affects the conditions of others in an inevitable downward path.[57] The damage, emphasise the trade unionists, also concerns honest companies that are penalised by unfair competition, and concerns the country in general when you consider the evasion of contributions connected with work on the black market. But careful – they say – responsibility for this situation does not lie with workers without documents but a system that does not allow legal entry. It may seem a completely unnecessary warning, but it is not, because anti-immigrant rhetoric assails a large proportion of the US working class, which continues to see them through the eyes of worker protectionism, as competitors in a race to the bottom and therefore to blame for their situation getting worse.

'When I hear these speeches I would like to ask: was it immigrants who relocated our factories? Or took away our pensions and health care? Perhaps it was immigrants who caused the financial crisis or decided on the commercial policies that destroyed so many jobs and companies?'[58] These are the questions posed by Richard Trumka, President of AFL-CIO, in an editorial on the CNN website entitled 'Undocumented workers need legal rights'. This is a new, strong position adopted by the trade union leadership. It is almost a manifesto, announcing the commitment to uniting the US working class, redirecting the politics of the fight between locals and migrants against the xenophobic cultural hegemony, which instead is aimed at dividing and opposing them. Trumka emphasises that in the US little is said of the many companies doing well from the system as it is, full of 'available and impoverished' workers. In short, it is a system with borders that are closed enough to change migrants into second-class citizens and open enough to guarantee an infinite supply of low-cost manpower without any social and legal power. All this, concludes Trumka, is 'intolerable for a democracy'.

Waiting for reform

The admission system in the US today is based on temporary visas for non-immigrants, tourists, students and fixed-term workers (the guest workers referred to previously), or permanent permits issued to immigrants for family or professional reasons. The annual quota of the latter is currently about 500,000 entries with a distribution of two thirds for family reunions and one third – 140,000 – for work. The rest go to refugees and permits drawn by lots in a real lottery. The permanent permit to stay, the green card, may be obtained after five years of residence (three if you are married to a US citizen or four if you are seeking asylum) and gives the right to request citizenship.[59] In 2010 more than 1,042,000 foreigners had the status of legal permanent residents, two thirds of them thanks to the family sponsor system. The countries of origin were Mexico, China and India. From 2000 to 2010 the average for permits of this type was a million a year, as opposed to 250,000 in the 1950s.[60] In 2000 the number of residents born abroad generally exceeded 10 per cent of the total (281 million) and new immigrants represented about half the annual increase in population, being concentrated in states such as California, New York, Florida, Texas, New Jersey and Illinois. The latest census, in 2010, shows that of the 312 million inhabitants in the US, the Hispanic community (16.3 per cent) managed to exceed the African-American minority (12.6 per cent)[61] numerically, and forms the majority in some large cities such as Miami, San Antonio and El Paso.

Illegal immigration, caused by illegal entries and temporary visas expiring, tripled in the last 10 years until it reached a peak of 12 million in 2007 to then fall to the estimated figure of 11.2 million in 2011. The Pew Hispanic Research Center[62] thinks there are about 8 million illegal migrants in the US workforce, these also in slight decline. These are obviously situations that have been created and grown up over decades, as a large proportion of these illegal immigrants entered in the 1990s and some even in the 1980s. They are Mexican workers in particular, about 60 per cent, followed by Central Americans and Asians.

The need for structural reform of the admission system is obvious, but the obstacles are many, starting with cultural ones. As already pointed out and as happens in almost every country of destination, the prevailing cliché is that immigrants are invading the US, benefiting from public social protection and taking work away from the locals, according to the slogan 'They take American jobs', which is often magnified by the media. Against the rhetoric on 'sponging' migrants, AFL-CIO points out that 'migrants come to the United States above all to work and not to get citizenship for their children'.[63] In fact the majority of those with children are active workers, more than 88 per cent. In spite of many of them living in situations of poverty, very few received the same support and benefits as indigenous US citizens. Furthermore, immigrants generate public wealth in excess of their cost in the long term. Various studies show that over the span of their working life, an immigrant pays about US$80,000 more in taxes than they receive in terms of state and federal services.[64] Therefore they give more than they take. Then there are some forms of assistance, such as Medicaid and Medicare health services and housing allowances, or forms of social security and benefits, which legal immigrants cannot obtain if they have not been resident for at least five years. With the exception of first aid and primary and secondary education for their children, undocumented immigrants are completely debarred from this whole section of the social state.

As far as the accusation of stealing jobs from locals is concerned, the historian Aviva Chomsky explains that the transformation of the US labour market – therefore unemployment in some sectors and the increase in insecurity – has more to do with the processes of deregulation and deindustrialisation started in the 1980s by the Reagan administration than the arrival of poor migrants from South America.[65] In fact, attraction factors continue to prevail over expulsion factors in migration between Mexico and the US because Central and Latin Americans are responding to the demand for flexible, badly paid work that US companies, and not only the private ones, badly need to stay competitive and remain on the market. The availability of so much migrant manpower, from building to catering, allows some Americans to maintain relatively low costs and devote themselves to better jobs, indirectly affecting the general productivity of the country, points out Alejandro Portes,[66] one of the sociologists who has studied the phenomenon of migration particularly in the US.

Migrants' children are also paying the costs of this situation because many of the new generation are often forced to live on the margins of society without any possibility of integration or social advancement. The children of resident migrants live trapped between the country and culture of origin, which they no longer identify with, and a society that refuses to accept and include them. Portes points out how in the medium and long term these conditions of 'downward assimilation'[67] will inevitably lead to higher levels of marginalisation, as already shown by the figures for abandoning education, social insecurity and potential new crime in the US. For this reason migration must be managed realistically and in a far-sighted way. AFL-CIO and the Change to Win coalition drew up a joint text where they mapped out their idea for reform.[68] The proposal consists of five points: setting up an independent commission to establish and coordinate future flows based on the real demand for labour; a secure and effective admission system; rational control operations on the borders; establishing the status of the population currently without documents; and improving – not expanding – the programmes for permits for a fixed time, limited to seasonal or temporary work. However, you need to go into the details of the text to read that they are also bringing up for discussion relations with Mexico, which has been penalised by NAFTA for too long; in short, this is an attempt to start a discussion that will be complex in its development, and not limited merely to the quantitative requirements of the labour force for the US. In any case it is all too clear that it is no longer possible to not take account of the universal application of regulations on work and social protection, the prime method for avoiding exploitation, social dumping and unfair competition. Instead the government is not making any progress, finding it difficult to set up a credible route for reform. In the elections in 2006 the Republicans lost many seats in the Congress, and the way the majority managed the matter of

HR 4437 did not weigh lightly. In 2007 President Bush failed again in his attempt to have a law passed that set up an amnesty route, but also restricted new work permits and extended the barrier on the border, with over 20,000 agents employed and millions of dollars spent on guarding facilities. In 2008, in the absence of any legislative guidance on a federal level, the governors started to regulate on the matter independently, creating 222 different measures in 48 states.[69] Most of these measures are aimed at discouraging immigration with restrictions on obtaining rights and social services.

In April 2010 the Governor of Arizona, Jan Brewer, signed a highly controversial law intended to reinforce the measures against illegal entries and to increase the repressive powers of the police, including the immediate arrest of anyone found without documents suspected of illegal migration. The law was criticised immediately by civil rights movements, given its highly discriminatory nature against Latin Americans, while jurists stressed its unconstitutional nature. Even President Obama declared he was against it, and the Department of Justice requested an injunction. In fact a federal judge stopped the measure the day before it was to come into force.[70] The state of Arizona appealed and in June 2012 the Supreme Court unanimously sustained the law's centrepiece, the so-called 'show me your papers' provision.[71] However, other measures were rejected, because they would have subjected undocumented immigrants to criminal penalties and this would interfere with the federal government's role in setting immigration policy. Since the Arizona law, five other states have enacted similar measures to halt illegal immigration: Alabama, Georgia, Indiana, South Carolina and Utah, even though they did not create new crimes for the violation of existing laws, as Arizona did with its provisions.[72]

In May 2011 the Development, Relief, and Education for Alien Minors (DREAM Act)[73] Bill, which would have allowed citizenship to be obtained gradually by about 65,000 children of illegal immigrants, was presented again, but not passed to the Senate. The Bill would apply to barely adult girls and boys, who arrived in the US as children, who had been resident for more than five years and had attended high school or enlisted in the army. Bipartisan congressionary groups had already presented similar measures to the

DREAM Act, but the Republican block always prevented their final approval. Only in 2011 in the states of California and Illinois were two laws passed ensuring access to university and the consequent permit to stay.

The challenge to the Obama administration today is to get a global immigration reform soon, centred on an efficient system of permits for qualified work, granting an amnesty for a large proportion of illegal jobs and reinforcing controls on the borders, avoiding legislative fragmentation but also the criminalisation of those without documents. In an inspiring speech on 1 July 2010,[74] on the subject of the amnesty, the African-American President said that the possibility of deporting 11 million people was simply unrealistic, and such an action would create a 'tear in the essential fabric of this nation, because immigrants who are here illegally today form part of that fabric'.

So far, however, concrete actions by Obama seem to have been few and disappointing in some cases.[75] The best thing perhaps has been the new policy put in place in June 2012 that would grant to young undocumented immigrants new work permits and immunity from deportation for two years at a time. The measure came after the failure of the DREAM Act and aimed to give a legal status to the over 1.7 million young people without legal papers, mainly Latinos, who arrived in the US before the age of 16 and who have lived in the country for at least five years. Also, Obama wanted the closure of some detention centres such as Hutto in Texas, where the families of the undocumented were held in prison conditions. The management of these centres has been completely privatised in the US, and security multinationals have made a multimillion business out of them. For the rest, however, the Democratic administration seems only to have continued the policy of the Republicans; in fact, during the Obama presidency, expulsions increased at a rate of 400,000 a year in 2009, 2010 and 2011, which is causing growing discontent in the Latin American community.

And for this reason the May Day movement has returned to the streets. In 2010 tens of thousands of people demonstrated against the law of Arizona. There were marches in 80 cities with the numbers taking part varying between 50,000 in Los Angeles and 65,000 in Milwaukee. "We have returned to organising ourselves for a big demonstration, but we have done so without a hierarchical structure, without sole leaders, this is a very heterogeneous, plural and decentralised network," explains Lee Siu Hin, a peace activist of Chinese origin and coordinator of NISN.[76] In 2011 the marches were held under the banner of 'May Day united' and with the slogan 'A day without a worker', stressing even more clearly the need to unite migrants and American workers, civil rights activists and trade union organisations. Under the pretext of the crisis and cuts in public spending, some states under Republican control, such as Wisconsin, tried to reappraise collective bargaining with the trade unions in order to reduce wages and contributions to pensions and healthcare. May Day demonstrations increased, as had not happened for years, from New York City to San Francisco. 'The truth is that migrants without documents and the public employees of Wisconsin have a lot in common,' sums up David Bacon. 'The politics which hunt immigrants are the same that want to dismiss state workers and wipe out any trade union protection.'[77] In the following year, with the slogan 'No borders between workers', a special forum was held at the AFL-CIO in Washington,[78] where union leaders from the whole American continent discussed the challenges of Latino and immigrant workers in the United States. According to Heli Vargas, from one of the Peruvian trade unions, "just as the companies are globalised to exploit us, the actions of the workers and unions must also be globalised as businesses are".

3

In France

Beyond the jungle

Once you arrive in Calais you're convinced that you've made it. You're in Europe and a step away from the UK, the goal of a journey that has lasted for months. The port, which is in the far north of France, is at the narrowest point of the Channel, only 33 kilometres from the English coast. The ferries shuttle back and forth and every day transport thousands of cars and lorries in just 90 minutes. Or there is the train, which goes through the tunnel, taking only half an hour. These times and distances are infinitely small for those who have travelled thousands of kilometres across Asia, Africa, the Middle East and the Balkans. Crossing the Channel is really nothing.

This is what the Indian boy must have thought, who was found by officers in the trailer of a lorry at the Port of Calais before embarking for the UK. They found him suffocated in October 2009. He was with two companions, who were still alive at the time the lorry was checked.[1] Like him, four other migrants died that year, all under 30 years old. The police continuously carry out inspections on both the French and English sides of the Channel and it is not difficult to flush out anyone inside the trailers. There is a device that detects the carbon dioxide produced by breathing; the boys knew this and put their heads in a plastic bag for each search so as not to be found. Rahmadin hid under the axle of a lorry instead, but fell near the Loon-Plage terminal in April 2010. He was 16 years old and came from Afghanistan. The same thing happened at the Grande-Synthe jetty in May 2011, when a 23-year-old Iranian hit his head after coming off the axle of a trailer. Martha, a 19-year-old Eritrean, escaped, but fractured her leg while trying to get onto a lorry.[2]

The stories are also similar to those from the border with Western Europe. They are stories that have been repeated for years and are happening in the ports of Patras in Greece or the Adriatic in Italy, but rarely end up in the newspapers. It is almost exclusively associations and volunteers helping migrants that document them, showing how serious they are. Médecins du Monde (MdM) is a French medical NGO that has been working in the Pas-de-Calais region since 2005. In its latest report, MdM denounced the conditions young people camped on the edges of the port are forced to live in, with 'no possibility of feeding, washing, clothing and sheltering themselves'.[3] The list of diseases and dangers encountered by migrants is long, particularly when they are trying to cross the Channel. A large proportion come from Afghanistan, Iran, Iraq, Somalia, the Sudan and Eritrea, countries tortured by conflict and violence. Many need protection, and European countries have an obligation to receive and protect them based on community directives and national laws, especially when they are minors, exposed to every kind of danger and abuse.

French officials of the UN High Commissioner for Refugees (UNHCR) comment that 'potential asylum seekers still find considerable administrative and bureaucratic obstacles' in Calais.[4] This is a euphemism for saying that they are certainly not encouraged to make a request for protection at the little French town on the border and most of the time they are left to fend for themselves, while trying desperately to reach the UK. They have been heading to the UK since their departure, certain of obtaining asylum, being able to work or study, integrating and starting to live again. Almost all speak a little English and say they have relatives and friends in London. For years the French and British governments have been discussing how to divide up asylum-seekers crossing the Channel. The 'Dublin II' European regulations, in force since 2003, establish that refugees must make their request in the first country of arrival and for this reason many push on illegally to where they believe it will be easier to obtain asylum and assistance, which is usually Northern Europe. These beliefs are often induced by traffickers, who have an interest in taking migrants further and further, continuing to make money from the journey in this way. 'Children are accompanied by someone saying they are an elder brother or an uncle, but in reality they are used to demand more money from the families,' explains Jean-François Roger of France Terre d'Asile (FTDA). 'They control the camps,' adds a volunteer, who has been working at the port for years, 'and they control access to lorries and trains. A boy who tried to get on a vehicle without paying the trafficker was stabbed in the side.'[5]

In 2002 the then Minister for the Interior Nicolas Sarkozy ordered the closure of the Sangatte centre to the south of Calais, run by the Red Cross. The purpose was to discourage arrivals and camps in the French town, but the migrants moved and spread to other areas in the region. They hid on the edges of inhabited centres in 'disturbing' sanitary and health conditions, according to MdM. The biggest camp, 'the jungle', as everyone called it, ended up taking about 1,200 people, who managed to survive thanks to the help of volunteers. One of the associations with the biggest presence is Salam, which has offered assistance, clothes and food since 2002. In October 2009 the then Minister for Immigration, Eric Besson, ordered bulldozers to demolish the tents and temporary structures. About 280 foreigners without documents were arrested, half of them minors. Among them was Najib Akhel Jabar, 12 years old, who had come from Jalalabad with a cousin of the same age. He told journalists from *Time* weekly that his father had sold a piece of land to pay for the journey to Europe, and to save him from the Taliban, who had wanted to enlist him for their war. Najib and his cousin had travelled for six weeks, hidden in the trailers of lorries across Turkey, Greece, Italy, and then finally France. Besson declared that all the minors in the camp would be held in an appropriate centre to then check for the possibility of asylum.[6]

Today in Calais a few hundred migrants remain, more and more scattered between camps, bridges, abandoned buildings and the dead-end tracks of the station. But according to a report by MdM, 'the police are not stopping at guarding and checking, but are going as far as destroying or confiscating migrants' property, personal effects or material distributed by humanitarian associations'.[7] This kind of tenacity causes contradictions between different offices of the same government. The Ministry for Health supports MdM, for example, and provides medical supplies. They have had to make the Ministry's logo on the medical kits distributed to MdM conspicuous to prevent the police from destroying them during round-ups in the camps. According to a report by the European Union Agency for

Fundamental Rights (EU FRA), French public health officials rely greatly on the work of volunteers, without whom migrants would not receive any form of assistance. Since 2004 the French government has also limited access to health services by illegal immigrants, in contrast with public service doctors, who instead ask for it to be open, not only for ethical but also for economic reasons. 'It is better to supply free preventive assistance,' they say, 'rather than resort to expensive emergency treatment. If the wait for treatment is then prolonged, it is possible that critical situations will deteriorate.'[8] The French government seems determined to carry on with the 'implacable war against irregular immigration', as Matthew Carr's article in the *New York Times* suggested.[9] And those paying the cost for this offensive are not only migrants, but also those trying to help them. The new regulations adopted by the Sarkozy government in 2005 dusted off and updated old decrees, laws and orders from the Second World War in order to make sanctions against anyone approaching an undocumented immigrant even more punitive. 'Anyone who by direct or indirect assistance makes it easy or tries to make it easy for a foreigner to enter, travel or stay illegally in France will be punished by five years in prison and a fine of 30,000 euros,' said the law.[10] In short, even solidarity has become a real crime. For Stéphane Maugendre, President of the Groupe d'information et de soutien des immigrés (GISTI), this article was written with highly 'symbolic' intent for the purpose of discrediting militants and associations.[11] In spite of Minister Besson trying to deny the existence of the 'crime of solidarity' by citizens and humanitarian organisations, there is no shortage of cases of volunteers being investigated for offering assistance. This is the tough and touching story told by Philippe Lioret in the film *Welcome*,[12] which shows how completely obtuse the laws are that criminalise undocumented migrants and those showing an interest in them.

Activists say they have also been pursued because of the campaign against Centres for Identification and Deportation. As happens in other European countries, anyone found without documents is detained awaiting deportation. In France there are 25 *centres de rétention administrative* (CRAs), and families with children are imprisoned in 11 of these.[13] Violence against detainees is not only moral, psychological and symbolic – explain the volunteers of La Cimade – but also physical, and it happens during deportation, when nobody can see. It happens during transfers or attempts at embarkation. There are doctors' certificates for migrants, who are examined on their arrival in the country of destination or when they are taken to the centre, confirming this.[14]

In 1977 Michel Foucault was highlighting the risks of the French security approach regarding questions of immigration and asylum.[15] According to Foucault, the 'security pact' governments have with their citizens should not lead to dangerous advances of power and distortions of recognised rights: 'We risk entering into a regime where security and fear challenge each other and build each other up.' In the face of a similar case to those currently linked to the crime of solidarity, Foucault wrote in an open letter to the leaders of the left: 'For millennia the private practise of asylum has been one of those lessons the heart of individuals has given to the States. Even if they do not listen, it would be unjust for these States to punish anyone proposing this practise to them, do you not think?'[16]

From the colonies to the *banlieues*

Among the European nations France was the first to become aware of the phenomenon of migration since the colonial era. It served in particular to bridge gaps in labour and to rebalance significant declines in the population. The reservoirs of foreign labour were first Belgian during 1800, then from Latin countries, such as Spain, Italy and Portugal, for almost the whole of the 1900s. Then, after 1960, migrants started arriving from North Africa, West Africa and the part of Asia that had known French colonisation. The ideology of the national state, which is highly centralised and secular, has always hindered the assertion of ethnic or local minorities, promoting instead a strong cultural identity built on formal recognition of the rights of equality, solidarity and fraternity confirmed by the 1789 French Revolution. In France, observes the sociologist Saskia Sassen, 'political values have traditionally played a greater role than heredity when it comes to membership of the nation'.[17]

For some time France has institutionalised the process of assimilation from both the legal and political point of view within its territory and the colonies. This process did not occur in other European nations that had known colonialism, such as Germany and Great Britain. For this reason the ethnocentric policies of France have made naturalisation easy through application of the principle of *jus soli* exclusively since 1889, even though the immigrant has always been considered 'a person without history and culture, ready to enter the great assimilating machine of French society as infinitely mouldable raw material,' as sociologist Umberto Melotti explains.[18] At the beginning of the 1900s and until the period between the two world wars, France without doubt had the most open migration policy in Europe and received refugees escaping from the Italian and Spanish Fascist regimes and migrant workers, predominantly from Italy and Poland. The demand for labour was high, and economic growth led the country to adopt progressive laws on rights, such as the eight-hour working day in 1919, before many other European countries. In the 1930s the foreign population in France was about three million.

Things changed with the crisis in 1929, which fuelled unemployment and increased the level of xenophobia among French locals until it came to mass deportations and restrictions on new entries. In spite of this being the nation that had received the most refugees during the Second World War, particularly from Nazi Germany, popular hostility towards foreigners grew stronger and stronger, and many limits were placed on their admission.[19] This was the period that saw a law passed punishing anyone making it easy for an illegal immigrant to enter and stay, taken up again 60 years later by the government of Nicolas Sarkozy and affecting pro-immigrant activists today. After the war, flows of migrants resumed both for reconstruction and for the phase of economic growth, attracting much labour from the ex-colonies of North Africa. The new recession in the early 1970s, which was partly due to the oil crisis in the Middle East, led to the almost complete stoppage of legal entries and various attempts at deportation and repatriation. 'Even in relatively open countries like France an attitude of opposition is spreading towards immigrants, who are seen as carrying a fearful threat of invasion,' notes Sassen.[20]

This 'invasion syndrome', which refers particularly to the Arab-Islamic share of new emigration, contributed to xenophobic reactions until the principle of citizenship based on territory of birth was brought up for discussion, with the result that the political forces of the extreme right proposed restoring the *jus sanguinis* in the early 1990s. The law was partly reformed by the conservative government in 1993 to then return to the *jus soli* with the centre left after the elections in 1997.[21] Regarding integration, which today is the real question at the heart of the debate on immigration in France, in the last 20 years immigrants have seemed less inclined to be assimilated by the national culture and identity, and a more pluralistic model respectful of differences has been asserted. Nevertheless, since the ethnocentric assimilation of the past, the model of inclusion is becoming fully functional today, determined by a mere economic means to an end, in a situation that causes contradictions and does not make integration easy for immigrants and their descendants.

The last census by the National Office for Statistics[22] indicates there are about 5,137,000 legal immigrants, representing 8.1 per cent of the active population. The number of permits to stay has already been severely reduced by the law of 2005, which Nicolas Sarkozy sought when he was Minister for the Interior. The *Code de l'entrée et du séjour des étrangers et du droit d'asile*, better known as the *Code des étrangers*, was imposed on the principle of temporary, functional immigration, immigration 'selected not suffered', according to former President Sarkozy. As regards the complete closure of the borders preached by the party of the extreme right, the National Front of Jean-Marie Le Pen, the Sarkozy law provides a system of permits to stay for a short time, to allow entry only to qualified workers, based on the economic requirements of the country, in the belief that the arrival of those without qualifications represents only an incentive to competition to bring down the labour market and therefore indirectly encourages xenophobia. The *Code des étrangers* also requires foreigners to have knowledge of the language and national laws. Restrictive measures have been applied to regularising the status of immigrants already on French territory, mixed marriages and family reunions, for the purpose of avoiding amnesties and discouraging new permits.

In such a climate of intransigence it is no wonder that in the same year, 2005, there was a series of uprisings in the French suburbs, the *banlieues*, where the descendants of immigrants live in conditions of marginalisation and are often subject to repression by the police. Similar episodes had already occurred in the 1980s and 1990s, but the intensity of the latest ones had no equal. 'In spite of town planning policies drawn up in the last 30 years, the situation of the *banlieues* has not improved: a heavy concentration of poor families, generally of immigrant origin, a high rate of unemployment, low level of education, lack of social services, crumbling council housing and lack of residential mobility due to the lack of an adequate transport system,' writes journalist Vincenzo Sassu in a book dedicated to the Paris suburbs. These are the conditions that caused an inevitable ethnic and social separation between the inhabitants of the *banlieues* and those of the city centre in a sort of 'soft segregation' in the French style, discreet, silent and underground.[23]

The tension that had been building up for years exploded in October 2005 following the death of two 17-year-olds in Clichy-sous-Bois, a suburb to the north-east of Paris. The boys were playing football on a building site and when the police, who had been called to investigate, arrived, they ran away because they did not have documents on them and knew they would have been detained. To escape the police Zyed Benna and Bouna Traoré, who were of Tunisian and Mali origin, ran to an electric power station and got into the transformer room, where they were electrocuted by a sudden discharge. The following day the Minister for the Interior at the time, Sarkozy, released a statement blaming the boys, as the police had only gone 'to prevent a robbery', he explained. The newspapers soon refuted the theory of the robbery, but the minister's attitude sparked a series of demonstrations. Sarkozy continued with his provocation: 'Are you fed up of this gang of "scum"? We will get rid of them as soon as possible.'[24] At that point peaceful marches turned into real riots, *émeutes*, inflaming whole districts, and not just in Paris. For almost a month scenes of urban guerrilla warfare with burning cars and smashed windows were repeated in another 200 French commenes, from north to south. The President at the time, Jacques Chirac, called a 'state of emergency' and the government mobilised more than 11,000 police, reinforced by the army. The protests slowly died down with hundreds of arrests, but the potential for conflict by those marginalised in the *banlieues* was by now obvious inside and outside France.

According to analysis by Alain Touraine, this degeneration was due to an important change that had occurred in the last few decades. The old liberal France knew inequality and conflict, but not urban ghettoisation, and its society had never been 'segregationist'.[25] The growing capacity for exclusion is now a characteristic of the new globalised society and this is helping to exacerbate conflicts wherever there are migrations and 'identifying' borders.[26] In fact, there seems to be a convergence towards the same model of exclusion and segregation of migrants in countries and regions with very different processes of economic, social and migration development, from the rich states of the Persian Gulf to the US and Europe.

The *sans papiers* and the workers

December 1972. In a church in Valence, south-east France, a chaplain of the Young Christian Workers and 19 Tunisians without documents began a hunger strike against the deportations threatened by a new ministerial circular. On Christmas Eve the parish priests of four churches in the town joined the protest and rang the bells to announce the first 'strike of the mass'.[27] The news soon spread to the whole nation and the support the protest received from public opinion drove the authorities to regularise the status of the 19 migrants.

It was the first reaction to the Marcellin-Fontanet circular, which was sought by the Minister for the Interior of the same name to stop the flows of migrants he called 'wild'. It was the years of the oil crisis and recession that as a result had driven the government to stop regularisation, creating a paradox, however, because those not accepted became illegal and those looking for work could not find it without documents. In May 1973 hunger strikes and church occupations increased throughout France, like that at Saint-Hippolyte in Paris.[28] One of the organisations most active in making demands was the Maoist group Mouvement des travailleurs arabes (MTA), which was the first to talk of the 'fight of the *sans papiers*'. To assuage the protest the government allowed another 50,000 regularisations between June and October, but also proposed a programme of assisted return to countries of origin, which few joined. In the climate of commitment and fighting for civil rights in the 1970s, demonstrations by immigrants received the support of civil society, French intellectuals like Jean-Paul Sartre and Michel Foucault, and trade union organisations, which started to recognise the social and economic role of the *sans papiers*.

Protests also went ahead in the following years with different groups of immigrants and refugees, while governments tried to restrict entries and remove illegal immigrants. Only in the early 1980s, with the Mitterrand presidency, did laws become less punitive, but only for a little while, because the executives of the right restored rigid measures that made it more and more difficult to work legally in France, until the right to citizenship on the basis of *jus soli* was brought up for discussion. The movement of the *sans papiers* returned to occupying churches and calling hunger strikes against this and other reforms in 1996. In June, national coordination was set up from the church of Saint Bernard, which gathered together 14 collectives and started actions throughout the country. In August the government sent 1,500 police to break up and disperse thousands of demonstrators, but the movement succeeded in obtaining a new amnesty, even though it proceeded more slowly, case by case, and not without a large number of deportations. At that point, the visibility of the *sans papiers* was such that migrants were present at major political and cultural events, from the Cannes festival to the sessions of the European Parliament in Strasbourg. In 1997 a group of 66 film makers and newspapers, including *Libération* and *Le Monde*, launched a petition inviting people to disobey the laws on immigration, and on 22 February there was a national demonstration with more than 100,000 people taking part. According to Johanna Siméant, who has reconstructed the dynamics and history of the movement, the decision to occupy churches was made for reasons that were partly symbolic and partly practical. Given the extra-territorial nature of churches, it would have been difficult to make arrests and deportations. Migrants without documents felt safe in church, and at the same time it was possible for them to appear and make their demands publicly and denounce their hardships. Through these actions, explains Siméant, foreigners were allowed 'to have a public existence, come out of the shadows and assert themselves'.[29] Nevertheless, similar demands would be more and more difficult with the closure of the borders and the denial of rights for all those daring to cross them.

As for the relationship that immigrant workers, regular and irregular, built up with the most powerful representative institutions making demands in France, the trade unions, for a long time there was a paradoxical situation, as the sociologist Maryse Tripier calls it.[30] On the one hand, foreigners represented the majority of the workforce in many sectors; on the other hand, they still lacked weight in terms of decisions and representation. The problem is in the idea of the migrant worker according to the still dominant model of the guest worker, borrowed from the German tradition of the *Gastarbeiter*, for whom the permit to stay is temporary and linked exclusively to the duration of the contract. The first generations of migrants in any country, not only in France, usually have no interest in integrating, and therefore in joining trade union organisations to take an active part in the life of the factory or workplace. Their interest is almost exclusively directed towards earning and then eventually returning to their country of origin. 'These people are at the centre of the productive system and at the same time outside the political and social system,' comments Tripier – it is as though they live beside the society to which they contribute. This exclusion is even more obvious if you think of the way towns are still divided between the town centre and the outlying districts, the *banlieues*. Since the 1970s the French trade union organisations started to include foreign workers, motivated in particular by the need for their support to succeed in disputes and only occasionally by idealistic reasons for integration and against discrimination. In any case, Tripier points out, for migrants, trade unionism remains the prime legal and legitimate channel allowing the whole of the French working class to take part and socialise, the prime form of recognition as 'people'. It is understood as a gradual process, requiring various limits to be overcome, even within a solidarity-based institution such as a trade union. If the French still find it difficult to accept, include and recognise foreigners, especially in phases of crisis and unemployment, foreigners' adoption of the values of locals is equally lacking. In fact, contact between locals and first generation immigrants is superficial outside the workplace and disappears completely if they are sacked or retire.

A similar tendency also contributes to the factor that is common to all industrialised countries – growing individualism among the locals – which leads to any form of collective demands being avoided. Migrants are not always prepared to fight, on the other hand. 'The demands of the immigrant worker, both those he shares with all the other workers and those he may put forward on his own account … ultimately are aimed only at reducing the constraint of work, in work and with work.'[31] The theory of Abdelmalek Sayad, an Algerian sociologist, is that the migrant lives in a state where he is completely outside the society in which he lives, as regards the moral and political dimension, in such a way that the only value work has for him is in connection with earning and wages. However, Sayad seems to be referring to the majority of first generation North African and African immigrants, those who arrived in France in the post-colonial period and saw the reality around them as 'complete chaos'. The cornerstone of this analysis is the figure of the general worker, *ouvrier spécialisé* (OS), the labourer, who seems destined to remain such for life, in a position of eternal subordination, as an immigrant, in the workers' hierarchy of the locals and society, without any possibility of integrating or moving up. In *Double absence* Sayad reports comments by some immigrants who were general workers: 'You're not taken on for what you can do, but for what you are … whether you're a Frenchman or an immigrant. It's not the same thing, it's not the same work, it's not the same pay. And when it's the same work it's never the same pay….They command, you must obey and keep quiet.You do.They command and so they can always not tell the truth.What's the truth? That all immigrants, particularly Arabs, must all be OS, for example, whilst no Frenchman has to be an OS.This is the truth, it's better just to say so rather than pretend we're all equal ...'.[32]

And yet, according to Tripier, just like the political analyst Immanuel Ness in the case of the US, today immigrants potentially have a great capacity for making demands, and this also allows trade union action to be revived. The conditions of exploitation they suffer and their greater inclination towards solidarity, and also the ease with which people and information circulate, knowledge expands and awareness grows in industrialised and developing countries, are all factors that may lead immigrants to revive traditional forms of class consciousness. These same forms that marked the history of the fight by workers in France in the past.[33] It is difficult to think of the marginalised and alienated Arabs portrayed by Sayad if you look at the example of the young men in the popular uprisings in North Africa, who overturned three regimes through spontaneous movements on the streets and social networks. The disputes in the last few years, starting with the workers *sans papiers*, show that this evolution in the history of immigration is also happening in France.

The reserve army in the kitchen

Le Monde describes him as 'a black and red trade unionist'.[34] Red because of his avowed, staunch Marxist faith, black because of his valiant defence of African migrants, the most exploited workers today – he says – even in France.

Raymond Chauveau is the coordinator of workers *sans papiers* for the Confédération générale du travail (CGT), the historic French trade union of the left, as well as its most representative. Since 2006 Chauveau has been involved in regularising the status of thousands of migrants, men and women, who actively contribute to a large part of the national economy, but who live in the shadows under conditions of constant insecurity and blackmail. At the heart of what he calls clear 'hypocrisy of the system', there are excessively restrictive laws on permits to stay for work reasons going to non-EU citizens.[35] Nevertheless, companies continue to employ workers, particularly with low qualifications, and people entering illegally are forced to accept any conditions without any contractual power. 'It is a mechanism that in the end harms everyone, not only immigrants,'[36] says Chauveau, because reserves of low-cost labour are created, which companies use to bring down conditions and wages. In short, for the trade unionist in France today a fundamental principle of Marxism still applies, 'the industrial reserve army'.[37]

Chauveau started work as a mechanical labourer in the mid-1980s in the RATP transport network of Île-de-France, the region surrounding Paris, and immediately joined the CGT. After he left the company in 1993, he became General Secretary of the Massy CGT in the department of Essonne, an area of *banlieues* still in the Paris region. For years – he says – the question of the *sans papiers* was considered predominantly from a humanitarian point of view and a large part of the attention was focused on the right to remain and live on the territory, but not on working conditions. The first exemplary dispute, in which the trade union sided with workers without documents, dates back to 2006, when 22 sub-Saharan workers went on strike and occupied the Modeluxe industrial laundries of Chilly-Mazarin. For almost two years requests for regularisation had not been listened to by the management and, faced with the threat of denouncement to the prefecture, letters of dismissal had been sent.[38] After initial hesitation all 160 employees of Modeluxe joined the protest, which went ahead for about a week with a certain resonance in the media, until documents were agreed for 22 migrants.[39]

"The workers understood that there would be no possibility of improvement for all employees without regularisation and real equivalence of rights," explains Chauveau. It was actually a first experiment to check the extent of this new movement and also focus on the role of the trade union. It was not a foregone conclusion that the organisation would agree to support illegal immigrants. At the start, "nobody was against it, but they weren't in favour either," admits the CGT coordinator. On the other hand, the trade union had also experienced the same hesitations and contradictions in its history when it tried to demand rights for other vulnerable categories, such as women workers, in the 1950s and 1960s.

Starting with this experience disputes increased and also extended to other sectors. Between May and June 2007 more than 50 African waiters and cooks went on strike and occupied the Buffalo Grill of Viry-Châtillon. The action went ahead for two weeks and was repeated in other restaurants belonging to the chain, again attracting the attention of the media and obtaining the support of other trade unions. During the days on strike the collective of the *sans papiers* wrote: 'Buffalo Grill has perfected the worst model of exploitation, which uses the vulnerability of illegal immigrants and does not respect their rights. It does not pay overtime, which makes up more than a third of hours worked, and keeps employees from any possibility of making demands.'[40] The political pressure was enormous, recalls Chauveau, because the protest occurred in the middle of the presidential election campaign. In the end, after meetings and negotiations with the prefecture, there were 23 regularisations, even though the other 40 employees had to wait the next big collective action in April 2008 to be regularised.

'I've been working here for nine years in the kitchen. Ten hours a day without a break. I'm either here or in another restaurant the owner has in Boulogne. We want a better life, for us and all the *sans papiers* in our situation. And we want to go all the way.'[41] Tama came from Mali in 1998 and is one of the nine cooks who shut down the kitchens of La Grand Armée restaurant, a prestigious place with a view of the Arc de Triomphe, on 12 February 2008, for a week. This strike also caught the attention of the French media, because it revealed a situation of widespread illegality and exploitation in one of the most exclusive places in the city, the restaurant frequented by politicians and celebrities, including President Sarkozy. Employment inspectors found legal contracts and documents, but in the names of other people, "a common practice for many restaurateurs," explains the unionist. Seven of the nine cooks had documents. Beyond regularisation, however, the value of this action lies in the fact that it was started by the immigrants themselves, showing that there was by now widespread awareness among the *sans papiers*, who were conscious that a large part of the economic activity of the capital was going ahead thanks to them.

Since then, mobilisation of this 'reserve army in the kitchen' has been extended and repeated throughout the Paris region at an almost monthly rate. Regularisations exceeded 6,000 in 2007, 12,000 in 2008 and 13,600 in 2009, arousing amazement and anxiety in the Sarkozy executive and among the employers, who counted on a certain indulgence by the authorities when faced with using labour on the black market. In 2009 more than 6,800 workers in the region went on strike, and mobilisation went ahead for eight months, with the result that a solidarity fund was set up to support families with no other source of income. Eleven trade union organisations, including the CGT, CFDT, UNSA, FSU and Solidaire, together with various associations, joined together in a collective to start negotiations with the Ministry for Immigration and the Department of Employment. The 'group of 11' presented about 4,000 dossiers and at the end of 2011 at least 3,000 were being regularised through the prefectures.

In May 2011 parliament also approved a new law on 'immigration, integration and nationality',[42] the so-called Besson law, named after the minister who proposed it. In theory the measure says that it wishes to stop work on the black market, offering illegal workers the possibility of obtaining wages and contributions, which were not collected, in compliance with national contracts. According to the trade unions, however, in practice it is rather complicated to apply the new regulations and to obtain anything. The law has been harshly criticised, particularly because it introduces even more restrictive measures for those entering the country without documents, with a longer period of detention and reduced access to legal assistance. As far as the workers are concerned, the principal challenge remains extending the regularisation, and in this way the obligation for companies to apply contracts, even for those categories that often remain excluded.

Take the case of the domestics, who were also involved in the strikes in 2009. The Droits Devant and Femmes Égalité associations turned up outside schools and nurseries to meet and inform all the home helps and carers who also live in situations of exploitation in France, which is all the more serious considering their isolation and invisibility. "Just because I have no documents, the mistress of the house thinks she can treat me like a slave," says a North African domestic. Her interview was reproduced in the report by the EU FRA on illegal migrants in domestic work.[43] According to the report, these *sans papiers* are exposed to excessive working hours, do not have days off or free weekends and are often subject to blackmail and even abuse. The threat to any attempt at bargaining is always the same: sacking on the spot without payment of wages and arrears.

The new socialist government, in power since May 2012, announced the creation of a new three-year work permit, but made it clear that it is not going to allow any mass regularisation of undocumented workers. However, the Minister for the Interior, Manuel Valls, announced various measures aimed at stopping the detention of families, at making regularisation criteria more uniform and at making naturalisation easier.[44]

"It is still soon to say if this government will act differently from the previous one," says Chauveau, "but it has to be noted that they are reconsidering some of the measures adopted in the past and they have asked for a dialogue on these matters with the trade unions and the associations." The unions have submitted a package of requests demanding also the involvement of the labour ministry.

Apart from exploitation, there is another worrying element for the trade union, which is linked to discrimination against legal immigrants. The experience with the movement of the *sans papiers* also drove the CGT to reflect on its role in representing migrants with documents – says Chauveau – who make up about 10 per cent of the workforce in any case. Even those who should officially have no problems, such as the descendants of North African immigrants, for example, are often excluded from the system. According to research by the International Labour Organization (ILO)[45] on the extent of discrimination towards second generation immigrants in France, the phenomenon is extremely widespread and makes equality of access to the labour market difficult. From a comparison between candidates who were the children of immigrants, and local candidates with almost identical CVs, specially trained to answer questions in the same way during job interviews, it appeared that young people of foreign origin had to answer an average of four to five more questions than the others to get a positive response in the search for a job. The highest levels of discrimination were found in the service sector and in small and medium-sized companies. In nine cases out of ten the choice between two candidates with the same characteristics, but of different origin, was made even before the employer had met the person, therefore being based simply on the name.

24h sans nous

> On the first of March 2005 the *Code d'entrée et de sejour des étrangers* came into force, a law with a unilateralist concept of immigration, based only on economic criteria. We could not have chosen a better date to call 'a day without immigrants'. We immigrants, descendants of immigrants, citizens who are aware of the contribution immigration has made to our country, are all consumers and take part in the growth of our country on a daily basis.

This is the introduction that opens the manifesto of the 'Une journée sans immigrés, 24h sans nous' movement, which was set up officially in September 2009 on the initiative of some French citizens and journalists, who had taken the US mobilisation in 2006, the Great American Boycott, as their starting point. The decision to form a collective and organise a national demonstration came after the xenophobic expressions of opinion by some politicians, both local and national, such as the ex-Minister for the Interior, Brice Hortefeux. In August he had commented before a young activist of North African origin from the UMP Party: "There's always one. When there's one it's all right. It's when there are so many of them the problems start." These statements drove a group of journalists and people from civil society to create spaces for open dissent on Facebook pages, gathering more than 50,000 members in a few days.

"This speech and the pathetic attempt to justify it were the last straw for us. Because it cannot be said that those statements aroused the indignation those offended wanted them to convey in public debate," comments Nadia Lamarkbi, a journalist of Moroccan origin and founder of the movement.[46] "We want to denounce speeches and portrayals aimed at stigmatising or criminalising immigration," she adds, "and prove instead that this is a resource for the economic, political, social and cultural enrichment of our country." In fact the alarms sounded by local politicians about the invasion of immigrants during the crisis were aimed at reinforcing the idea of foreigners as 'opportunists and parasites' as regards the public benefits system. According to surveys in that period, more than 63 per cent of the

French thought that the debate on national identity was not very constructive and only encouraged the stigmatisation of immigrants.[47] The setting up of the Ministry for National Identity (incorporated by the Ministry of Interior in 2010) was subject to criticism by progressive forces and trade union organisations.

According to the sociologist Eric Fassin, as in the case of the US demonstration, mobilisation in France had to 'play on the active continuum' between irregular and regular migrants. After all, maintains Fassin, there is no real opposition between 'us' and 'them'; rather immigration runs through the history of a country as a continuum, in the US and in France.[48] Having chosen the date for abstaining from work and consumption, the 24h sans nous collective sent an open letter to President Sarkozy, inviting him to go on strike, since he was also the child of immigrants, they recalled ironically. In reality his parents' situation was quite different from that of the workers *sans papiers* – Sarkozy's father was a Hungarian aristocrat and his mother was descended from a rich family from Salonica.[49] Nevertheless, when the *Code des étrangers* was approved by the Minister for the Interior, someone had also joked about the fact that his father would never have been able to enter France with such a measure.

The movement immediately described itself as apolitical, not incorporated into any organisation, refusing any party label, but gathered members from various associations defending human rights and some trade union organisations, including Solidaires and the CFDT confederation, which was traditionally close to social democratic forces. The absence of the CGT was cause for discussion, with the result that some local branches decided to join independently. At that time the CGT was heavily involved in the dispute regarding the major regularisation of almost 7,000 *sans papiers* and there was a fear that taking part in 24h sans nous would have distracted attention and caused confusion about the reasons for the strike. In any case, organisation of the day of boycott, which was set for 1 March 2010, went ahead via the website, meetings, conferences and promotion in the media. On the site of *Libération*[50] the collective emphasised the open and inclusive nature of the movement, which was formed not only by immigrants, regular and irregular, first and second generation, but also by French citizens 'in solidarity'.

The demonstrations took place peacefully on 1 March in various towns in France, recording about 7,000 people taking part. This was not mass mobilisation. "Taking part was symbolic," admits Lamarkbi, "we wanted to change ideas about immigration and make people aware of the essential contribution immigrants make to our country. I cannot say whether there were more immigrants or French people. We are not interested in measuring results in this way." It was actually predominantly a cultural movement that had a certain media impact, not only in terms of coverage in newspapers and on television, but particularly in terms of members through the great resource of the internet and social networks.

This experience shows how in a few weeks it is possible to bring together and put into contact tens of thousands of people and to contribute to the public debate on such a controversial subject. Unlike the US movement in 2006, mobilisation in France does not seem to have involved foreign workers, because the migrant population in Europe does not have the same uniformity of language and culture as the Latin American population in the US. The US demonstrations of 1 May also benefited greatly from the support of religious groups and of the Catholic Church. Above all, however, the US movement had a specific purpose, which was shared by a wide coalition of forces: stopping the new law by the Bush administration. The activists of 24h sans nous are still there on Facebook, and in the following two years there were new demonstrations in Paris with the slogan: 'Tous libres et égaux en droits' ('All free and equal in rights'). Nevertheless, the impact of the movement has been less than at the start and all the social capital generated by the first initiatives could have been put to better use.

France has a long tradition of fights against racism and for the rights of minorities. However, these initiatives do not always include the youth and might be politicised, Lamarkbi remarks. "Our movement offered young people the possibility to express themselves beyond the political divisions and with new, different kinds of action, in particular with flash-mobs, concerts and debates in cafés."

In fact, today there is a great need for a cultural movement against xenophobia in France, which requires a broad alliance to be built, including all the associations defending migrants and refugees together with the workers *sans papiers*, coordinated by the trade unions. In essence there is a need for a heterogeneous, plural movement of opinion, a true multitude that succeeds in bringing together the invisible immigrants in Calais, those in detention centres and those in Paris kitchens. And not just them.

In July 2010 the Sarkozy government decided to dismantle 300 Roma camps thought to be illegal, and adopted a security plan that provided for the 'voluntary' repatriation of about 700 Roma of Romanian and Bulgarian origin in three months, with individual incentives of €300. The 'behaviour of some of those belonging to the Roma and travelling communities' was the pretext for what several parties have called ethnic-based collective deportation. According to supporters of the opposition, the Roma were used as an easy scapegoat and instrument of consent to distract public opinion from the political failures of the government in view of the 2012 elections.[51] After an initial demonstration of condemnation, the European Commission decided to renounce disciplinary action against France, but remained firm in its criticism of the measure. For the French authorities it was a question of public order, while according to Community regulations there is no threat to security. And any deportation can never be generalised for an entire community.

Although the new President, socialist Francois Hollande, had openly criticised the deportations ordered by Sarkozy, the dismantling of Roma camps went on in the summer of 2012, as did the repatriation of Roma people to Eastern Europe. Human rights groups and some progressive political forces accused the government of further discriminating against the Roma and criticised the executive for not having offered any alternative to resettlement to the families living in the dismantled camps.

'France must send a clear and strong signal throughout Europe to reaffirm human rights and dignity for all individuals,' wrote Benjamin Abtan, president of the European Antiracist Movement, in an editorial for *Le Monde*. 'To recreate its own image and to strenghten rights equality in Europe, it's urgent that today France marks a clear difference between now and the actions and the spirit of 2010.'[52]

4

In Italy

The Mediterranean wall

They did not all die of asphyxia, as was first thought. Some were beaten to death. The coastguard found 25 bodies in the hold of the boat coming from Tripoli, among about 300 Somali, Ghanaian and Nigerian migrants rescued off the coast of Lampedusa during the night of 31 July 2011. Some worrying facts about the dynamics of the events and the responsibility of the people smugglers have already emerged from the first accounts by the survivors: 'They shouted to get out through the trap door but were thrown back down. They asked for help because they had no oxygen. One of them managed to get out through the trap door but some men took him and threw him into the sea, where he drowned.'[1]

Part of the group was forced below deck, where there was also the engine, for fear that the boat, which was only 15 metres long, would capsize. It was useless to protest and try to get back on deck. For days the Italian media kept coming up with the image of those bodies lying on Favarolo jetty in Lampedusa, one beside the other, wrapped in blue plastic bags. They were all very young and there was also a woman among them. The first results of the autopsy confirmed deaths not only due to asphyxiation and carbon monoxide fumes from the engine, but also from violent beatings. According to the report by the police doctor, one of the victims had a fractured skull in two places and another had fractures to the cheekbone and forehead.[2] The Department of Public Prosecutions in Agrigento arrested the six alleged people smugglers on the boat, one of whom was Moroccan and the others Syrian and Somali, accusing them of encouraging illegal immigration and the crime of murder as a result of another offence. According to the magistrates, they had acted 'with cruelty for despicable reasons'.[3]

The survivors, including 36 women and 21 children, said they had passed another five boats with just as many migrants aboard. New boats arrived during the hours and days that followed, loaded with people fleeing from war-torn Libya and people escaping from other conflicts, particularly in the Horn of Africa. As with migrants at the Port of Calais, at the border of Lampedusa there are potential asylum-seekers, forced to leave their countries. It is a situation that has been repeated for at least 10 years and now makes the Mediterranean one of the principal asylum routes.

The Fortress Europe website has been following the dynamics of flows of migrants towards Europe for some time, and collecting information on every landing and shipwreck it can trace. From 1988 to the summer of 2012 it estimated that at least 18,350 people died trying to cross European borders, from the Straits of Gibraltar to the Aegean Sea. From 1994 to 2011 in the Sicilian Channel alone at least 5,962 people lost their lives, more than 4,500 of whom are still missing.[4] In the Mediterranean too the numbers are those of a 'war against immigrants'. 'The routes go from Libya, Tunisia and Egypt to the islands of Lampedusa, Pantelleria and Malta and the South East coast of Sicily,' they explain at Fortress Europe, 'but also from Egypt and Turkey to Calabria.'

Although attempts to reach the Italian coasts went down significantly from the beginning of May 2009 to the first few months of 2011, they have not gone down as a result of wars in Africa ending or fewer people fleeing. During this period the Italian government adopted a policy of 'push-backs' on the high seas, based on an agreement with the Libyan government in open violation of the right to asylum (which provides for rescue at sea and identification). For almost two years those managing to escape the chaos in the Horn of Africa found themselves trapped in Libyan detention centres, where they could make no request for protection, since Libya had never signed the 1951 Geneva Convention on the right to asylum.[5] According to Human Rights Watch, the Libyan authorities kept records of refugees detained in centres and allowed officials from the most sanguinary governments, such as Eritrea, to identify their dissidents, which exposed them and their families to the obvious risk of retaliation. 'Italy is responsible for the people it has rejected in

Libya, a country that does not provide asylum and brutalises migrants,' declared Bill Frelik, Director of the Human Rights Watch Refugee Programme.[6] But any appeal to the government remained unheard. Italy, on the contrary, had every interest in maintaining good relations with these dictatorships. According to various investigations by *Espresso* weekly,[7] the Italian government and the Lombardy Region had a series of ongoing business deals with the Eritrean authorities, ranging from weapons to construction. And yet the UN had placed an embargo on Eritrea with a resolution by the Security Council because of the logistical and military support given by President Isaias Afewerki to the Al Shabaab terrorist organisation and other groups allied to Al Qaeda in Somalia.

The agreement on push-backs was also criticised by UNHCR, as it undermined access to asylum in the EU, violating the fundamental principle of non-rejection contained in the Geneva Convention on refugee status, the legislation of the EU and other international conventions on human rights.[8] Information shows that until then, those landing on the Sicilian coasts had been people fleeing from conflicts and violence: 'Before 2009, over 75 per cent of those arriving in Lampedusa made a request for asylum and the Italian State recognised a form of protection for 50 per cent of those people,' explains Laura Boldrini, Italian spokesperson for the UNHCR.[9]

The policy of rejection met with no opposition from the European Commission, however. Rather than intervening in the causes of African conflicts, which were also exacerbated by economic and food crises, the Commission invested exclusively in hindering measures, patrolling the coasts in the Mediterranean through Frontex and agreements with Libya to stop migrants and asylum-seekers. In October 2010 the Commissioner for Internal Affairs, Cecilia Malmström, signed an agreement with the Gaddafi government to finance greater activity to control the southern borders of Libya in the desert, allocating €50 million and being limited to asking for the laws on asylum to be brought into conformity.[10] In essence this was a contract to unload the problems of forced migration more and more on the south, out of sight of Europe.

The Arab Spring and the conflict in Libya brought all previous agreements up for discussion and journeys resumed at an even more sustained rate, but this time driven by the Libyan government. 'The landings have a commander. He is called Zuhair Adam and he is a high ranking officer in the Libyan navy. The information comes from a rebel stronghold and is confirmed by the accounts of all those arriving in Lampedusa these days,' wrote Gabriele del Grande, founder of Fortress Europe, in his blog on 10 May.[11] The regime, which was under siege by rebels and NATO (North Atlantic Treaty Organization), had understood that sending migrants could be a good strategy, a form of retaliation against Italy, from where military aircraft took off. Therefore it closed the border with Tunisia, where refugees from Libya had poured over until then, and started to organise crossings at the cost of more than €700 per passenger. In this case too, as in South East Asia, on the border between Mexico and the US, or France and the UK, migrants are doubly exposed to violence, extortion by traffickers and the risk of dying in attempts to cross a border.

For those managing to reach Italy, however, the war was not over. During the years of the last Berlusconi government, from 2008 to 2011, there was an exponential increase in episodes of violence against migrants and minorities, predominantly Roma, often culminating in tragedies. Since 2007 the Lunaria association has been trying to monitor the most significant stories and collect them in the Chronicles of Ordinary Racism report.[12] The long, thick 'inventory of intolerance' presents dozens of attacks from the north to the south of Italy. In December 2009, in Zumaglia near Biella, a 35-year-old Senegalese construction worker, Ibrahim M'bodi, was beaten to death by the owner of the company he worked for, Franco D'Onofrio, because he had claimed three months' wages in arrears. D'Onofrio tried to get rid of the body by throwing it into the drainage channel of a paddy field.[13] Local and national newspapers gave little importance to the news, apart from *il Manifesto* daily, which dedicated its front page to it. Ibrahim had a brother, Adam, leader of the FIOM CGIL metalworkers' union,[14] who had tried to mediate with the businessman. After the murder the Biella trade unions organised a base in front of the prefecture of the town as a sign of protest.

Another two symbolic cases show how attacks are not only motivated by racism, but are also linked to a deeply rooted, generalised system of exploitation of labour. The first occurred in September 2008 in Castel Volturno in Campania, where six boys from Ghana, Liberia and Togo were slaughtered in cold blood by a commando unit of the Casalesi clan, a Camorra Mafia cartel. Hundreds of shots were fired along the Via Domitiana, leaving six on the ground and seriously injuring a seventh. Via Domitiana is a long street where migrants are recruited by illegal hirers at dawn for a day in the fields or on building sites. The reason for the massacre was that the Africans had refused to pay protection money to the Camorra men and not – as some newspapers wrote originally – accounts being settled between the Campanian underworld and members of the Nigerian Mafia, who now control part of the local market in drugs and prostitution. Almost all the African boys had arrived by sea, passing through Lampedusa, and some through Spain, but not before going through the desert and often Libyan prisons.[15] The day after the massacre the migrants decided to go onto the streets of the town, tired of being treated like criminals and by the police taking no action in the face of continuous abuse. There was an outburst that saw them breaking shop windows and overturning cars while shouting 'We want justice.'[16] Investigations and anti-Mafia police operations led to the arrest of more than a hundred members of the Casalesi clan, including the head of the wing that carried out the massacres, Giuseppe Setola, who was tried and sentenced to life imprisonment.

The other story took place in Rosarno, Calabria, in January 2010. On their return from the fields three labourers from Togo, Morocco and the Ivory Coast were hit on the legs by bullets from a compressed air weapon. There was nothing new about the attack. Africans are ideal victims of the criminal world that runs orange picking in that area of Calabria, often intimidating them to avoid paying them. The same thing had happened in December 2008. Then the migrants reported it to the police, showing courage and a sense of civic duty in a territory where the code of honour and conspiracy of silence prevail, as Antonello Mangano wrote in the book provocatively entitled *The Africans will save Rosarno*.[17] That evening in January, however, the migrants did not stop at reporting, but went into town and started overturning dustbins, clashing with the police. The next day the protest carried on and tension mounted, causing a response by the citizens of Rosarno that soon became out of control. Armed with clubs and sticks, the citizens formed patrols and seriously injured several Africans, pursuing them to their homes, which they then set on fire. In a sort of collective hysteria, a 'black hunt' started,[18] which required intervention by the police and mediation by local pro-immigrant associations and the UNHCR. The police had to remove the Africans and take them to a reception centre to save them from the fury of the citizens. And they were not even illegal immigrants; most had documents. Many were in Rosarno because they had lost their jobs in companies that were in crisis in the north, and others were refugees.

The events in Rosarno, which were magnified by the media, highlighted the squalid conditions these boys were forced to live in, and brought new accusations of barbarity and racism raining down on Italy,[19] causing subsequent misgivings by the international community about the policies of the Berlusconi government. These events also caused indignation among millions of Italians, who could not identify with this show of xenophobia. Some days after the events in Rosarno, in an editorial in the *New York Times*, the writer Roberto Saviano commented: 'In Castel Volturno immigrants work in the building industry. In Rosarno they pick oranges. But in both places the mafia controls all economic activity and the only ones with the courage to rebel were the Africans.' And he concluded: 'To those immigrants I say "don't go away", don't leave us alone with the mafia.'[20]

Between amnesty and security

It is well known that in the last few decades, like other nations of Western Europe, Italy has gone from being a country of emigration, both internal and external, to a country of immigration. Unlike countries in Northern Europe and like Spain, Portugal and Greece, Italy has stopped exporting workers since the early 1970s, starting to recruit them instead from developing countries, first from North Africa in the 1980s and then from the Balkans and Eastern Europe after the fall of the Berlin Wall in 1989. Migrants came not only due to the expulsion factors of poverty and underdevelopment, but also due to attraction factors – rapid economic growth, demographic change, women coming onto the labour market and a new organisation of the welfare state.[21]

Ratification of ILO Convention 143 in 1981, which was aimed at stopping illegal immigration and protecting workers against discrimination, must be remembered as one of the first interventions to regulate entries for work in Italy.[22] The first important amnesty dates back to 1982, however, which inaugurated a policy destined to be repeated over time due to the difficulty of providing and managing flows with the new mobility of labour. Since 1990 immigration has started to be considered a question of national interest and security, not only economic and social. The first law dealing with labour and asylum matters in a structural way was in 1990.[23] This also provided an amnesty but introduced the obligation of a visa for almost all countries of origin, and started the policy of deportation. Two years later, in 1992, the law on citizenship was approved, introducing the ethnic criterion for determining the national community, according to the principle of *jus sanguinis*, with citizenship also being extended to Italian descendants who had emigrated abroad.[24] While legally resident EU citizens could be naturalised after four years, for non-European foreigners the time limit was moved from five to ten years.

The Consolidated Text on Immigration dates back to 1998[25] when the centre left was in power. On the one hand it set up temporary detention centres for the deportation of illegal immigrants, and on the other hand tried to make the admission and integration of legal workers easier through the system of quotas and 'sponsors'. The centre right government of 2002 started a new amnesty, the fifth and perhaps the greatest until then, with more than 702,000 requests, and modified the Consolidated Text through Law No 189,[26] known as the Bossi-Fini Law after the names of the two ministers signing it, the Northern League leader Umberto Bossi and the post-Fascist Gianfranco Fini. The new measure reinforced controls, made entry quotas more discretional and discouraged taking on foreigners legally, removing the sponsor and reducing bilateral agreements for preferential quotas. This rigidity did not solve the problem of work on the black market; rather it seems only to have contributed to the illegality and insecurity of foreigners.[27] The sole substantial merit of the law was decentralising the asylum procedure and setting up 10 territorial commissions to examine requests for international protection.[28] Quotas of permits to stay for work, established from year to year through the Flows Decree, are currently low and limited to seasonal work or care work for home helps and carers. And yet the need for foreign workers in all economic sectors is now evident. According to a study by the Ministry for Employment,[29] in the 2011–15 period, the foreign labour that Italy needs amounts to about 100,000 people a year, while by 2020 the annual quota will have to go up to 260,000, well above what has been provided so far by decrees. It begs the question why, if the demand for foreign workers is so great, more realistic criteria are not adopted for setting quotas and more legal permits are not granted.

The cliché of immigrants stealing jobs from Italians is not enough to explain this contradiction. Studies by authoritative organisations such as the Bank of Italy[30] confirm that foreigners do many of the jobs Italians no longer want to do, and their presence allows local people to dedicate themselves to better jobs. So in the current Italian production system there is a labour market reserved almost exclusively for immigrants,[31] and foreigners are now essential for the survival of many businesses and entire sectors, from Tunisian fishermen in Sicily to Sikh animal breeders in Puglia, from Filipino nannies and home helps in large towns to Moroccan stone carvers in Trentino.

The most recent information from the Caritas Migrantes dossier[32] indicates that there are more than 4,571,000 foreign citizens legally resident in Italy. In particular they are Romanian, Albanian, Moroccan, Chinese and Ukrainian. More than half are women and overall they represent 7.5 per cent of the resident Italian population, less than in other European countries like Spain or Germany. According to estimates there are about 540,000 undocumented immigrants, but there are more than two million working legally, about 10 per cent of all the workers employed and 3.5 per cent of company owners. Together they produce 11 per cent of national GDP. The most significant fact is that 'they pay in more than they take out,' according to Caritas and based on information from the social security agency, INPS,[33] because every year they provide almost

€11 billion for the state treasury, while they cost a lot less in terms of allowances and services.

In spite of the evidence of numbers, immigrants continue to be victims of violence and racism, as shown by the stories at the beginning of this chapter, in both industrialised and agricultural areas. There is no doubt that this is largely attributed to the political class that has governed the country in the last few years and built its identity and electoral success on fear of the foreigner. It is enough to quote the ex-Minister for Internal Affairs, Roberto Maroni of the Northern League, who on several occasions declared the need to be 'tough on illegal immigrants' or 'clandestini',[34] denigrating and blaming anyone arriving in Italy without documents, taking no account of motivation. It was no less than the ex-Prime Minister, Silvio Berlusconi, who openly declared his opposition to a multiethnic society.[35] In short, the years of right-wing governments have been years of open war against immigrants, in words, policies and practices.

The most determined opposition has come from abroad, from European and international institutions worried by growing levels of racism and discrimination in Italy. The Commissioner for Human Rights of the Council of Europe, Thomas Hammarberg, has been making observations regarding the treatment of immigrants, asylum-seekers and Roma since 2009. International NGOs, such as Amnesty International and Human Rights Watch, have done the same. And there has been no shortage of criticism from the Vatican and UN agencies, from the UNHCR, which has already been quoted regarding the policy of push-backs. The ILO criticised Italy harshly for violating Convention 143 in relation to discrimination against migrant workers through its Committee of Experts.

According to a report on immigration and the trade unions by the IRES CGIL,[36] this discrimination is above all institutional due to lack of access to public employment, from which non-EU workers are excluded, a situation conflicting with the 1998 Consolidated Text on Immigration and European directives on equality of opportunity among other things. There is also no recognition of academic qualifications and professional experience, their contractual status is lower, less protected and lower paid (on average 24 per cent lower in comparison with Italians),[37] and overtime and some important allowances are often not paid, leaving aside training and safety issues, two elements considerably increasing the probability of accidents at work and occupational diseases. In general the fact that the permit to stay depends exclusively on the employment contract according to the guest worker model in Italy also makes immigrants more insecure and open to blackmail, but above all it leads to a form of self-discrimination, driving them to passive acceptance of any kind of treatment.[38] The offensive against undocumented migrants reached its peak with the adoption of the 'security package' in July 2008. The declared intention of the government was to 'stop illegal immigrants and illegal immigration more effectively'.[39] For this reason 'the offence of being illegal' was introduced, which considers illegal entry to be a real crime, and 'the aggravating circumstance of being illegal', which punishes those guilty even more harshly if they are non-European without documents. According to the majority of legal interpretations, the regulations have a highly discriminatory nature because the accused is no longer assessed based on the offence committed, but on status.

In international law it is not acceptable for a migrant entering irregularly (often because he is the victim of trafficking) to be considered by the law to be a criminal as well as his trafficker. The new regulations in Italy have ended up encouraging situations of exploitation because migrants without documents will be driven to move away from almost any form of legality, relying only on criminal organisations for entry into the country, staying and working. However, the European Directive on Repatriation that came into force at the beginning of 2011 imposed a series of modifications to the Security Decree. In fact the removal of illegal migrants requires individual assessment, case by case, and not the indiscriminate application of deportation practised by the Italian authorities. In February 2012, three months after the fall of the Berlusconi government, the European Court of Human Rights in Strasbourg condemned Italy for violating the European Convention on Human Rights because of its policy of push-backs on the high seas of people in need of protection. Such a policy is clearly unlawful and can no longer be adopted to manage migration flows in the Mediterranean. 'For sure this ruling reminds the current government that the agreement with Libya has to be reconsidered,' commented Laura Boldrini, spokesperson for the UNHCR, 'in order to get over that policy and give a sign of discontinuity, which has fallen short so far.'[40]

What would happen?

'What would happen if the four-and-a-half million immigrants living in Italy decided to down tools for a day? And if the millions of Italians who are tired of racism supported their action?'

This is the provocative question that was used to present the manifesto of the First of March, A Day Without Us movement in Italy in January 2010. It started two months after the French movement of the same name, and was inspired by the US movement from 2006. The manifesto stated: 'We are immigrants, second generations and Italians, united by the rejection of racism, intolerance and closed attitude characteristic of Italy today.' The objective was to organise a large, non-violent demonstration and strike via the internet and social networks to make public opinion understand how decisive the contribution of immigrants was to Italian society's existence and functioning. One of the founders was Stefania Ragusa, a Sicilian journalist living and working in Milan: "We met in a very informal way and decided to open a page on Facebook and a blog together with other immigrant friends, a Cuban trade unionist and a Senegalese businesswoman, or Italians with direct experience of immigration because they are married to foreigners."[41]

The blog included a series of instructions for those wanting to set up a local committee, requiring them to be not only individual initiatives but also in a group, preferably with knowledge of the territory and the organisational capacity to mobilise a certain number of people, migrants and Italians together. All this activity developed very quickly with progress in making contacts continually and constantly growing, particularly after the Africans' riot in Rosarno. The movement immediately received support, and therefore legitimacy, from a large part of the anti-racist world, from major associations like ARCI and Legambiente to Emergency and PeaceReporter, which offered headquarters in Milan as well as the support of Coordinamento Migranti, individual priests, some missionaries and even Cobas trade unions. The relationship with the major trade union confederations was more difficult. The CISL and UIL national secretaries made it known from the start that they would not support the demonstration, while there was an attempt at liaison with the leftist CGIL. "We met to see if it was possible to cooperate," says Ragusa, "but their conditions included putting the demonstration into the programme of initiatives for the Anti-racist Spring and also abandoning the strike. Relations were more constructive with some branches, like the metalworkers of FIOM. At the same time a request to take part came from the Trade Union Centres in the territories and the Immigration Offices of the trade union, which workers were turning to because they wanted to support the strike."

In fact some leaders of the confederations called the initiative of the First of March 'ethnic' because it divided rather than united workers, therefore conflicting with trade union principles of solidarity and universality. The CISL in the Veneto region, for example, produced a press release,[42] saying it was 'useless to support a strike launched through Facebook by people who have never been moved to protect foreigners'. 'Strikes called during the electoral campaign,' it said, 'tend to divide subsequently and move away from social cohesion, which is cultivated every day, not with initiatives characterised by political advantage.' A CGIL national secretary, Morena Piccinini,[43] declared that the initiative was a 'strategic and political' error, because you needed to think about how to unify the fight and mobilise the whole world of work regarding the rights of migrants.

Other trade unionists admitted that there was a problem with immigrants being represented within organisations, and proposed a different argument. Dino Greco, ex-Secretary of the CGIL of Brescia, launched the idea of a mass discussion in every workplace. Otherwise, 'if migrants come to believe that their diversity is an obstacle to full equality within the trade union,' he said, 'they will end up going other ways.'[44] The organisers of the First of March rejected the accusation of wanting to divide workers with an ethnic strike, and the claims that there was no distinction between immigrant workers and Italian workers, and that the demonstration concerned everyone, not just immigrants. They knew perfectly well that the movement had no right to call a strike action and requested support from the trade union for this reason. The initiative went ahead with the support of numerous human rights associations and the support of magazines, newspapers and political parties of the opposition, including the Democratic Party.

In Italy about 300,000 people took part in demonstrations, with marches filling many squares from Milan to Rome, from Naples to Palermo. The result was remarkable considering the speed with which the demonstration had been organised, the complete lack of structure and the lack of a strong link with major political organisations and trade unions. The economic impact was also in proportion to the spontaneity of the movement. Some metalworking, textile, food and chemical factories closed where trade union representation units had officially announced the strike day. This happened in areas where the trade union had a greater presence and where there was a high concentration of immigrant workers. These included: 48 factories in the province of Brescia, 6 in Bologna, 7 in Parma and 12 in Reggio Emilia.[45] Small businessmen also went on strike, as, for example, in Turin at the Porta Palazzo market, which remained closed to the surprise of local citizens.

A new national coordinator, Cecile Kashetu Kyenge, a doctor of Congolese origin, was elected, and a political document came out after the movement's national assembly in September 2010. Since then the movement has focused on some programme objectives, such as undertaking to 'recognise the right to full citizenship of those born, growing up, living and working on the Italian territory', passing from the principle of *jus sanguinis* to that of *jus soli*. Other objectives were the right for immigrants to vote at local elections, creating equal opportunities and the rejection of special laws, as well as creating an information campaign about CIE detention centres, literally Centres for Identification and Expulsion. The demonstrations and activities by local committees were repeated in following years with partial support by the CGIL, but fewer people took part in marches and strikes. In 2010 it was the emotional impact of the events in Rosarno and the media attention these events gave to the migrants' reasons that contributed greatly to mobilisation. "The realistic objective of the new demonstrations was to keep up the tension and attention on the elements characterising the project," explain the organisers, "grassroots mobilisation and the central nature of some watchwords, like clear opposition to the Bossi-Fini law, defence of rights in work, the mixed nature of society and the strike as a tool for mobilisation and protest."

Among the different questions raised by the Italian anti-racist movement is one that has appeared most forcefully in the last few years relating to the right to citizenship and the right to vote. In 2011, the I'm Italy Too campaign started, which brought together 19 organisations, including the Democratic Party and the CGIL. Through committees set up throughout the country more than 50,000 signatures were collected for two popular bills needed to reform the 1992 regulations on citizenship and to give the right to vote to immigrants who had been resident for at least five years. The President of the Republic, Giorgio Napolitano, openly said he was in favour of *jus soli*.[46] However, the strong majority of centre-right forces in parliament prevented attempts to turn these bills into law.

From factories to the crane

The province of Brescia is one of the most industrialised areas in Italy but is also where discrimination against foreigners, who represent a considerable part of the labour force, is strongest. Local governments, which are predominantly centre right (People of Freedom and Northern League), seem to take every opportunity to blame immigrants and to fuel prejudice about the threat to citizens' security. In October 2009 the Diritti per Tutti (Rights for All) association denounced the highly discriminatory nature of a series of fines imposed by the municipal police of Brescia, such as the one against a Moroccan lady because she was sitting at the foot of a monument, the one against two workers drinking a beer outside a pub and the one against Asian boys playing cricket in the park.[47] A month later, in the town of Coccaglio, the councillor for security, a Northern League supporter, started the White Christmas operation with the objective of removing undocumented immigrants by Christmas Day, which was understood as 'the celebration of Christian identity and tradition'.[48] Municipal police went to inspect the homes of people from outside the community to check the status of their permit to stay, with the threat of revoking residence if it had expired, until 25 December.

In April 2010 Adro Town Council denied access to the school canteen to children from families who had not yet paid their fees, who were mostly foreign. In May the same mayor of Adro, a Northern League supporter, decided to limit some forms of benefit just to EU citizens, such as the rent fund and the baby bonus, a measure that was immediately blocked by the labour judge because it was discriminatory and was then condemned by the Brescia Court of Appeal.[49] In October Gavardo Town Council gave the go-ahead to a census of homes in the areas where immigrants lived with inspections by municipal police to check on health and safety and to issue a questionnaire for landlords and owners, which was clearly aimed at discouraging renting to foreigners. Direct intervention by the prefecture and the monitor of the National Office for Racial Discrimination (UNAR), which called it conflicting with 'the principle of equality of treatment',[50] was necessary to stop the measure.

In such a context you can understand why the proposal for a day of mobilisation by immigrants, on 1 March 2010, immediately met with a favourable reception. The local anti-racist network had already been working for some time against the discriminatory orders of local governments. Support for the 'strike by foreigners' came from Moroccan, Pakistani and Sri Lanka communities, Italian associations such as Giustizia e Libertà, the political parties Sinistra Ecologia e Libertà and the Democrats, although the local CISL and UIL trade union confederations and also Caritas kept their distance. Since the initiative had been openly criticised by the national secretaries in Rome, the Immigrant Office of Brescia CGIL discussed the need to support the movement with the provincial secretary. Driss Enniya, a Moroccan who had been in Brescia since 1989, where he was also a delegate for the metalworkers' FIOM, was running the Office. "We felt obliged to give our support because these immigrants had already expressed the desire to demonstrate and strike but didn't know how to manage such an action or what risks they would be exposed to without the intervention of the trade union," recounts Driss.[51] "I explained to the secretary that the train had now left and that these people would have gone on strike without us. What would we have done after that? Our leaders understood and they let us act independently. I must say they showed courage."

Forty-eight union representatives supported the strike in as many companies, from Cromodora in Ghedi to Tomo Gomma in Bedizzole. Production stopped for eight-hour shifts and support by the workers was almost total. And not only by migrants, who represented 40 to 80 per cent of those employed in many companies in the province, with an average of 100 employees each. More than 20,000 metalworkers are registered with the CGIL in Brescia alone. Workers marched in line wearing blue overalls, highlighting that it was not only 'illegal', unemployed immigrants who were demonstrating, but legal workers with awareness, workers who wanted their own voice to be heard. Local government politicians tried to delegitimise and denigrate the demonstration because it had high visibility in the media and saw so many Italian citizens taking part, with whole families coming together in the march to then join the concert in the Piazza della Loggia.

There were also businessmen who openly declared their support for the protest because they understood that the strike was not against them but against the laws on immigration and the bureaucracy surrounding the permit to stay. A determining factor for including so many people was relations with the local media and the use of social networks, because they involved many more citizens. Cohesion and coordination between ethnic groups also made a major contribution. "The Sri Lankans, in particular, showed they were well organised and connected with all co-nationals on the territory," says Louise Bonzoni, a Brescian activist of the First of March. "But many Pakistanis, Moroccans and domestic workers from the East also marched and even the Chinese who have shops."[52] The most resistant, those least interested in making claims, were the new EU members, Romanians and Bulgarians, who viewed the arrival of new migrants with a certain 'protectionism' and adopted closed positions, even politically. As for the rest, the request to take part was clear and found a response in the network of associations and trade unions.

In Brescia, 1 March 2010 was just the first of a series of demonstrations for migrants' rights. At the end of September a permanent base was set up against the new regularisation by a group of Egyptian workers in front of the prefecture. The 2009 measure was only intended to regularise the status of home helps and carers, excluding hundreds of thousands of workers who were employed, but on the black market. It also provided a payment of €500 to the social security national agency, INPS, by the employer for each employee to have their status regularised. But after a year the amnesty that everyone was now calling 'the amnesty scam' had proved to be ineffective, as about 10,000 people had made a request without receiving documents and false employers had deceived many others.

The protest became even more dramatic at the end of October, when six immigrants of various nationalities climbed up a 35-metre crane on the Metrobus site in Brescia to protest. For 17 days there were clashes and attacks by the police against the demonstrators under the crane, there were arrests and deportations, institutional negotiations started and failed and there were attempts at mediation by the trade union and even the Church of Brescia.[53] These did eventually serve to persuade the migrants to come down, after the authorities promised to examine the cases and reconsider the possibility of permits. Among the deportations, that of Mohamed El Haga, who formed part of the base group under the crane, is symbolic.[54] Mohamed was stopped in the middle of November 2010 while he was trying to prevent the deportation of another nine migrants. After being taken to the Centre for Identification and Expulsion, he was kept in isolation and finally deported to Egypt. The authorities in Cairo held him at the airport for three days and then released him with a ban on leaving the country or province of residence without permission. Only in March 2011 did the Regional Administrative Court of Milan accept the appeal that Mohamed had made against the rejection of his request for amnesty. But it was too late.

Meanwhile, at the same time in Milan, another eight immigrants supported the action in Brescia, occupying the tower of the Carlo Erba ex-pharmaceutical factory. They came down after 27 days, on 6 December. Among them was Marcelo Galati, an Italian-Argentinian, who became the leader and symbol of this occupation in spite of not having any problems with his own permit to stay because he was of Calabrian origin and this gave him the right to citizenship as an Italian descendant. In the radio documentary by Marzia Ciamponi and Ebe Giovannini,[55] Marcelo recounted that this demonstration had been organised together with migrants in Brescia, and the occupation of the crane and the tower represented just the start of a much wider protest, uniting migrants against a law that only encouraged exploitation. "The amnesty scam," he says, "is confirmation that in Italy they don't want to regularise the status of anyone, they want to create a class, a vast group of people in a state of slavery."

The farm labourers' strike

Work starts at three in the morning when the hirers go and collect the labourers in vans. They get up to 25 in a vehicle with 10 seats without windows. The labourers do not know the way from the farmhouse to the field, so they are forced to take the vehicle owned by the illegal hirer, who wants €5 for transport, just like he wants money for food, €3.50 for a sandwich. Everything is deducted from the daily pay for piece work. It is little more than €3 a box, which weighs between 400 and 550 kilos and takes an hour or more to fill, depending on how quick you are.[56]

This is what happens in the Puglian countryside, where every year in summer migrants pick tomatoes and melons. These same migrants then move to Calabria to pick oranges, like in Rosarno, or nearer places in Campania, according to the season. They work without gloves and without any safety measures or assistance if there is an accident. When someone is hurt, they try to call for first aid, but they cannot even give directions to the field where they are, and the illegal hirers take advantage of this. They want another €20 to take them to the nearest hospital.[57] This account comes from Ivan Saignet, 26 years old, from Cameroon, who arrived in Italy in August 2008 with a visa to study at the Polytechnic of Turin, where he got a degree in telecommunications engineering. In 2011 he decided to go to Nardò in Puglia, for the melon season, to earn money to pay towards his university fees. "The first day I had to sleep on the ground because the tents were already occupied by my companions, that was a shock, I had never seen such a thing, not even in Africa."

In the northern part of Puglia, like in other areas of the countryside in southern Italy, agricultural work seems to follow the same rules and customs as from the beginning of the 20th century, when labourers were Italians. In spite of time passing and in spite of changes in society and the Italian economy and major fights and victories by the labour movement, the system of exploitation is carrying on just the same, with the labourers at the mercy of the illegal hirers, the 'overseers' of the past, who 'regulate, manage and control the work of new slaves,' writes journalist Alessandro Leongrande.[58] Today these slaves come predominantly from sub-Saharan Africa and North Africa, but they are also new EU members, Polish, Romanian and Bulgarian, all different, with different motivations and aspirations and often divided and even more open to blackmail for this reason. On the other hand, the illegal hirer has also become multiethnic over the years. "Apart from Italians, there are various Ghanaians, Nigerians, Sudanese and Burkinabes, as well as North Africans and Eastern Europeans," recounts Ivan.[59] This diversification allows groups of labourers to be managed better and, it is assumed, controlled better. A practice common to all of them, however, is withholding documents. As soon as workers arrive, they are asked for their original documents with the excuse that they are to be used to write contracts. In reality the permit to stay are kept in the hands of the illegal bosses for weeks, and during this time the same documents are reused for illegal immigrants, if and when there are inspections. In the end the contracts are false and legal migrants are stuck, unable to move or go away because they have no way of showing that they are in Italy legally. This is no different from what happens in the US countryside with Central American guest workers. In this case large food companies also completely rely on the illegal hirers and do not know or do not want to know what really happens in the fields and what conditions workers are kept in.

In 2011 in Puglia, however, something happened that seems destined to influence this unchanging cycle of abuse. In the same summer that Ivan Saignet went to Nardò, the labourers decided to rebel, but with a strategy and specific objectives. In August, under the pretext of low prices for watermelons, the illegal hirers started demanding higher work rates to get more boxes of fruit a day, otherwise – they said – they would not pay anyone. At that point the situation became insupportable for the labourers. They formed spontaneous committees and held the first meetings. About 400 migrants were housed in the Boncuri farmhouse, which was provided by the commune of Nardò with the assistance of volunteers from the Finis Terrae and Brigata di Solidarietà Attiva associations, which were already involved in the 'Sign me up against work on the black market' campaign.[60] Their demands were coordinated by FLAI CGIL trade unionists, the organisation for agricultural and food workers, which for more than two years had been setting up bases in the area and reaching migrants in the fields. It is the "street trade union", as it is called by Stefania Crogi,[61] FLAI General Secretary, because it is difficult for migrants to go to trade union centres due to understandable fear, diffidence or simply because they did not know that there was a trade union.

This is how activity to make people aware of their rights started in an attempt to involve as many workers as possible. The first difficulty was linguistic, because migrants spoke different languages: Arabic, English, French and some only African dialects. Therefore a committee was created, made up of different representatives, one per community, which explained the reasons for the protest to the various groups and the way in which this would be organised. The demand was for higher payments and a legal contract directly from the companies, or the workers would strike. And that is what happened. In spite of threats and intimidation by the illegal hirers, the fields remained deserted, the vans remained at a standstill and the migrants demonstrated in the streets, stopping traffic on the main roads. Together with FLAI trade unionists they went to the prefecture with a platform of claims, starting with compliance with the provincial labour contract for agriculture, which had a specific rate for picking: about €6 an hour and €38 a day. "There was a new awareness, immigrants arrived at a conscious decision to fold their arms and go on strike and without doubt this decision represents an important turning point," explains Crogi. The protest in Puglia also served to shed light on the worst situations of exploitation, which had been neglected by institutions and authorities for too long. The words of the Public Prosecutor of Lecce, Cataldo Motta, on this subject are significant: 'Immigrants have given us a great lesson in civilisation, showing that you need not be afraid of denouncing crimes and when denouncement becomes unanimous, any risk disappears. Italians should do the same, laying bare usury, extortion and all illegal acts committed by organised crime.'[62]

The strike went ahead for 13 days until the middle of August, with results going beyond the local dispute. The Puglia Region decided to start encouraging those demanding and those supplying labour to meet, with the objective of getting round the illegal hirers acting as middlemen, in agreement with the companies and trade unions. Reservation lists were created, where labourers could be registered and then be employed directly by the companies under legal conditions. The lists were put up in public places, which were open to everyone, such as the town hall, employment centres or the farmhouses where workers lived. The trade union is now trying to replicate this system in other regions, such as Emilia Romagna and Lazio, since local government is now responsible for a large part of regulation of the labour market.

Above all, however, the protest in Nardò speeded up the implementation of a new national law, in August 2011, which makes being an illegal hirer a criminal offence.[63] The measure arose from a bill presented by opposition parliamentarians, in particular deputies and senators of the Democratic Party. "This is a very important tool for us, a decisive step forward," explains Stefania Crogi, "even if it is still being completed by penalties for companies using illegal hirers, benefits for proper companies and measures to protect those making denouncements." Illegal workers, who are the most exploited, cannot be certain to report illegal hirers because they would risk being involved in another offence, that of being illegal, which could lead to their immediate deportation from the country. "We have done a lot," says Ivan, "but we must continue to fight, provide information and awareness campaigns, otherwise the illegal hirers will continue with their activity as before and the first step is the new law, to make it more effective." Apart from the legal aspects and developments, what is striking about Nardò is the political aspect of the conflict that was triggered. This fight has the merit of having built up a dense network of solidarity throughout the region, it shed light on the limits and incapacity of institutions to face up to the structural questions of Italian agriculture and certainly represents an important moment, not only in the history of migrant labour, but the whole workers' movement in Italy.

The development of the conflict in Rosarno also shows that a new awareness is spreading among migrants in the south of Italy. Two years after the famous clashes between citizens and Africans a demonstration was held in the small Calabrian town that saw anti-racist associations come together with groups of Gioia Tauro dock workers, immigrants picking oranges and activists from social centres. 'For the first time there is a new working class made up of blacks and whites, which is developing self-awareness,' writes the journalist Valentina Loiero, 'with foreign workers taking part in the fight of the Gioia Tauro Plain and Calabrians supporting battles for the rights of foreigners.'[64] Only two years have passed, but they seem like 20, comments Loiero. Associations offering assistance to foreigners, Africalabria and Equosud, have managed to get some labourers taken on with legal pay of €40 a day. But there are still many, too many, who continue to live and work in the same conditions as before, for little more than €20, living in isolated houses without water or light in many cases. On the other hand, the citrus market is such that many small owners have been forced to sell off fruit or underpay labour, that is, when it is not actually more expedient to leave it on the trees.[65]

'I don't work for less than €50 today' was written on the placards of the migrants' movement in Castel Volturno in October 2010. Two years after the massacre by the Casalesi, the African boys decided to protest again, but this time they demonstrated on the roundabouts where the Campanian illegal hirers come to take them to the building sites at dawn.[66] The very place of exploitation was chosen symbolically as the place to relaunch the fight, which in Italy has assumed a much wider significance, and concerns a whole generation in insecure work. In fact the same slogan was chosen a few months later for a campaign by freelance journalists, who are paid a few euros per article and in turn risk their lives to denounce abuse and violence in these territories that are controlled by organised crime.

5

The mobility of labour

Need for governance

National migration policies have so far failed. The stories collected in this book and many others happening every day show the complete inadequacy of what is a unilateral, temporary and often repressive approach to mobility. Thousands of men, women and children are continuing to die on the borders, with just as many suffering violence if they do manage to get across. How sustainable is the current migration system in the long term? What is the international community doing about it? How can we manage migration realistically, giving people both dignity and safety?

The migration question has certainly not been resolved by militarising borders further or by reducing visas and permits to stay. Movements of people are increasing in frequency and happening within a highly developed network of social and economic relationships. A global phenomenon like contemporary migration cannot be left to the decisions and solutions of individual states, let alone the political agenda of parties. In a recent study,[1] the Migration Policy Institute (MPI), a research institute based in Washington in the US, highlighted the limits of current policies, and put forward a series of proposals, the crucial point being to develop effective cooperation through regional agreements within the scope of multilateral relationships between industrialised countries and developing countries. However, the greatest problem remains the attitude of governments, particularly those of the richest and most influential countries, faced with the possibility of the global governance of migration and therefore the transfer of power over their borders and the conditions under which migrants stay on their territory. This is a paradox, as governments see this coordination as necessary, but at the same time as unattainable. And some countries of origin also seem to be rejecting common, binding rules because they are afraid of the impact on remittances from migrants, which is a prime source of wealth for their economy. There is no doubt that the first step towards effective cooperation is to adopt and apply clear, shared regulations, although the principles laid down by existing international conventions concerning economic migration have not met with systematic support from states through ratification and national laws or support within society through popular consent. And yet, there is no other way of providing protection and rights for migrants in a uniform way on a global level than to combine principles and supranational reference regulations with building up consent in individual countries. According to the MPI analysts, this can also not be done by proceeding with an institutional approach from the top, or simply through a formal multilateral system, because flows of migrants arise from the interaction of informal networks, from the bottom and on bilateral or regional routes. Therefore the organic development of existing systems in policies and practices, including the informal type, must be respected. The supranational structure under consideration is something other than the institutions or agencies imposed by the richest countries, such as the International Monetary Fund (IMF) or the World Bank are for movements of capital, and the World Trade Organization is for movements of goods and services. Some other critical observers[2] would also like the approach by the UN system to be rethought, which so far has been limited to creating coordination between its agencies in the Global Migration Group[3] or establishing the Special Representative of the General Secretary for migration and development. These decisions continue to have a purely consultative and non-binding value for governments, they say, which does not resolve current imbalances.

Interventions by agencies and organisations in charge of various aspects of contemporary migration have not resolved the problems either. The Office of the High Commissioner for Human Rights (OHCHR) is the principal UN office mandated to promote and protect human rights, and speaks out against human rights violations. The United Nations High Commission for Refugees (UNHCR) deals exclusively with asylum-seekers and refugees, for whom it also provides protection by working with governments to apply the 1951 Geneva Convention. As for economic migrants, the main reference point could be the ILO, which sets international labour regulations according to the 'Decent work agenda'[4] and constantly verifies the application of those regulations by member states. The International Organization for Migration (IOM), which is not part of the UN, mainly helps governments to manage migrants in a practical way, from reception to repatriation. All these organisations involved with migration also produce a lot of research that they use to advise governments, but none has the role of coordinating or directing national or regional policies, let alone carrying out a function that is binding on individual states.

The first attempt to start down an inclusive, multilateral route, involving various players such as UN agencies, groups defending human rights, governments and trade unions, is the much wider Global Forum on Migration and Development (GFMD),[5] which was set up in 2006. The Forum is connected to the UN system through the Special Representative of the General Secretary and has created a 'platform for partnerships' with the aim of exchanging information on various policies and cooperation projects. Those taking part also include representatives of the International Trade Union Confederation (ITUC) and of the Global Unions Federation (GUF) which focus their attention on economic migration and on the idea of temporary work according to the 'guest worker' model. 'The temporary approach is a simplistic one that has proved to be ineffective and is also being reconsidered because often it represents only a way of getting round laws and protection,' declared Sharan Burrow, ITUC General Secretary.[6] From the perspective of a place to start the ideal governance of migration 'in practical and action-oriented ways', as the GFMD aims to, transnational trade union organisations could have a decisive role and may make a difference if they succeed in receiving and coordinating demands by migrant workers, which otherwise run the risk of remaining fragmented and unheard.

The migrant nation

The most recent estimates of the UN[7] indicate there are about 214 million international migrants, 3.1 per cent of the world population. If they were a nation, it would be a bit bigger than Brazil and a bit smaller than the US. If family reunions, forced migration by asylum-seekers and evacuees, and illegal immigrants (about 10 per cent of the total) are excluded, there are about 105.4 million who could be called economic migrants or global migrant workers,[8] these also being equal to about 3 per cent of the overall labour force. This is a percentage that has remained constant over time, at least in the last 40 years, and explodes the myth of invasion in recent years.

The other cliché relates to the direction of movements as from the whole of the South to the North, while in actual fact flows are now much more mixed. The number of migrants going from the poorest countries to the richest (South–North interregional movements) is just over a third of the total, equal to those moving within these regions in South–South or North–North intraregional movements. Of the eight-and-a-half million migrants from West Africa, for example, only a million reach Europe (640,000) and North America (350,000); all the others remain on the continent.[9] The most recent trend is the movement of workers from South East Asia, sub-Saharan Africa and Latin America to emerging countries like Brazil, India and China, or from Central Asia to the Russian Federation, while the advanced economies of Europe and the US, those most affected by the 2008 economic crisis, are increasingly less attractive due to either high rates of unemployment or restrictive policies on new entries.

Unlike migration in the past, today the numbers of workers with medium to high levels of education are also increasing, who are characterised by leaving and returning frequently, every two to five years, following a more circular model of mobility. These include many students and young professionals, who travel to economies with specific programmes for settling in, predominantly in the scientific, information technology and financial sectors, but also as doctors and paramedics. Another new element concerns the type of migration, because the so-called 'feminisation' of migration for work is growing and today represents 49 per cent of the total, with women unquestionably being in the majority in care services. Women are becoming more and more the protagonists of mobility and of the economy, either because they are breadwinners who provide resources for their families, or because they are 'first migrants' who start migration chains and reunion processes.[10]

Beyond expulsion and attraction

To try and find the direction these changes are going in it is useful to consider how the factors causing movements combine today and whether there is still a traditional distinction between push and pull factors. In neo-Marxist literature on the theory of dependence,[11] geographical inequalities in development processes, caused by colonial and neo-colonial exploitation, form the basis of contemporary economic migration. This theory is backed up by information on persistent economic and social imbalances and the inversely proportional relationship between world population and wealth,[12] since most of the population, about 80 per cent, continue to live in the poorest countries, demographic pressure is high and the Human Development Index is low.[13] Another explanation is based on unemployment and under-employment factors, which predominantly concern developing countries. A demand for low-paid work in developed economies corresponds to a lack of stable and secure work in developing economies. On the other hand, attraction or 'pull' factors are associated with the 'dual theory of the labour market', which is supported by Michael Piore, a US economist.[14] In Western countries development has not removed unstable, unhealthy and unqualified work, so-called '3D' work,[15] 'dirty, dangerous and demanding', nor insecure and unprotected work, which is particularly widespread in agriculture, the building industry, heavy industry and services, including care services. This sort of work no longer attracts local people, so demand can only be filled by unemployed or under-employed immigrants. According to Piore, the labour market ends up divided into two: the prime market has better conditions and is reserved for locals, who are better protected, and the secondary market has worse conditions and is reserved for the weaker and more insecure, predominantly immigrants. In reality there is a tendency to admit that there is a convergence between these factors, which are becoming integrated, also taking into account new elements, such as the revolution in communications and transport in the globalisation process, as well as the role played by networks of transnational relationships between immigrants.[16]

These interpretations would not be complete if they did not also include individual motivation, the capacity and desire for choice by immigrants, not necessarily assuming they will remain passive when faced with difficult structural conditions. In trying to bring about convergence between the theories, between the structuralist and the individualist approach, the most recent studies have concentrated on the role and action of social networks, relationship networks between immigrants and potential migrants and networks establishing 'social bridges' between countries of origin and countries of destination. As far as the previous theories are concerned, the other assumption is that 'the decision to migrate is not made in a vacuum without social relationships'.[17] This perspective highlights the increasing dynamism of migrants as social players, connected in networks, proving to be variable irrespective of the level of wealth of the countries of destination and restrictive measures of a political order. The 'transnationalist' approach centres on analysing the figures for 'transmigrants' who develop social networks across borders and move in the changeable relationships between capital and work.

Globalisation without development

A trend in new international migration is the increasingly ephemeral distinction between countries of origin, transit and destination, and there are many countries that represent the three different dimensions at the same time, as shown by the examples of India and Mexico. The North African region, Eastern Europe and Southern Europe, to some extent, are also countries migrants leave to go to Northern Europe, where some pass through and some, who come from sub-Saharan Africa, arrive and settle. The softer demarcation of borders and greater frequency of movements and returns for short periods make contemporary economic immigration a much more fluid phenomenon and in many cases circular, compared with previously, particularly if it happens within social and family networks, which make arrival and return easier.

Doubtless this fluidity has been made easier by the global economic process that has a specific relationship with international migration, a relationship based on natural mutual influence. In fact globalisation tends to fuel international migration in the first place, due to the increasing circulation of information. Thanks to the development of technology, better and more frequent possibilities of contact spread a feeling of 'relative deprivation' in the populations of countries at an intermediate stage of development, where information and communication are more accessible, which drives migration even more than poverty itself.[18] The expansion of means of communication, but also of trade and tourism, in the poorest countries produces a sort of 'socialisation in advance', the attitudes and behaviour of the societies they are going to already being acquired to some extent in the societies migrants are leaving, which motivates and encourages them to leave, avoiding a stressful impact of different cultures and customs, as would have happened previously.

A higher level of education also contributes to this form of socialisation, particularly on a linguistic level, so that any geographical distance progressively ends up not corresponding to the cultural one. Globalisation has produced a revolution in transport, which makes intercontinental movements much more affordable. The expression '3T', which refers to innovations in 'transport, tourism and telecommunications', is often used to indicate the effects of globalisation on international migration.[19] To these elements must be added being able to carry out economic and financial transactions more easily to transfer useful sums of money quickly and securely to those migrating for economic reasons.

Reciprocity also has an influence on globalisation processes, which are understood as an increase in exchanges and economic interdependence. The greater availability of immigrant labour in industrialised countries, for example, constitutes an alternative to exporting production to countries with low labour costs and an essential resource for jobs it would not be possible to export, such as in the tourist sector, building industry and personal services. The companies and activities of immigrants increase the supply of services in the countries of destination from sectors of the legal economy to the informal and even illegal economy in some cases. Immigrants contribute to internal demand increasing in the countries of origin through remittances and to economic development processes starting from the bottom. From a cultural point of view migrants returning to their countries of origin bring with them the values and behaviour they have acquired in the countries where they have lived, contributing to these forms of uniformity a sort of 'market multiculturalism', which represents one of the principle characteristics of globalisation.[20]

Where do resources go?

As far as the relationship between mobility and development is concerned, on an ideal scale economic migration should contribute both to reducing poverty in the countries of origin and to supporting the economy and wellbeing of the countries of destination. In reality there are many negative effects, however. Apart from the conditions of exploitation migrants find in the countries of destination, the loss of precious resources, both material and intellectual, in the countries of origin must also be considered. While academic literature and studies by international organisations abound with information on economic remittances, there is little information on the specific mechanisms allowing – or preventing – growth and development in the countries of origin.[21] Regarding remittances, the first difficulty with analysing them is quantifying the amounts of money transferred from countries where people go and work to those they have left, because only part of the money goes through official credit systems, in view of bank charges and a commission for transactions. According to estimates by the World Bank, however, the sums sent home by immigrants rose from US$62 billion in 1990 to US$417 billion in 2009.[22]

The 2008 financial and economic crisis has also had a severe impact on remittances, which for the first time in decades suffered a reduction, estimated at about 10 per cent, although the fact remains that they are more stable compared with the reduction in private and humanitarian funds intended for development. Whether they are official or informal, remittances continue to represent a vital resource for the economy of the poorest countries, the main source of income, which is three times higher than international donations.

The countries that benefited the most in quantitative terms in 2009, for example, were India, China and Mexico, even though the greatest effect on GDP was recorded in small countries such as Tajikistan (35 per cent), Lesotho (26.2 per cent), Nepal (23.8 per cent) and the Republic of Moldavia (22.4 per cent).[23] The advantage of remittances is that they generally benefit family members of workers who have emigrated in the poorest sections of the population, who managed to get out of a state of extreme poverty, financing education for the youngest and care for the elderly. More problematic is the question of redistributing remittances from families to the community, from individual consumption to investment in economic forms that could encourage development. In fact the problem of economic and social inequality is associated with the failure to share resources, also causing a sort of 'mythologisation of remittances' as the principal cure for poverty, a real culture of migration[24] that drives the youngest to leave with no interest in the local labour market.

The resources generated by workers who have emigrated are not limited to money, but also include all the social practices, knowledge and skills they have acquired while living and working in a richer country, which are shared and used for development in the communities and societies of origin on their return. Only then can you talk of 'social remittances' according to the well-known definition by Peggy Levitt: 'while individuals communicate their ideas and practises to others in the role of friends, relatives or neighbours, in their function as organisational actors, they also communicate in their capacity as organisational actors, which has implications for organisational management and capacity building'.[25] Levitt also underlines the importance of the capacity migrants bring from their country of origin to the country of destination. Beyond returns and the possible advantages of remittances, when migration does not represent a necessary alternative to unemployment all the negative effects are felt in the countries of origin. These concern in particular the loss of labour resources, both manual and intellectual, the phenomenon generally known as the *brain drain* and the *care drain* in care work. In the case of intellectual resources the loss for the poorest countries is even more serious, if you think of public investment in education and training, particularly in sectors with a strategic role in getting out of underdevelopment. There are countries in sub-Saharan Africa, for example, that supply doctors and nurses to European nations like the UK, leaving hospitals behind without the professional people needed to prevent and cure the most widespread diseases. The way the richest countries take away precious human and intellectual resources from developing countries is a controversial subject and, in defining the governance of sustainable mobility, the need for better programmes aimed at the return of professional people after a period working abroad, and also for training younger people, is undeniable.

The other resource families in the South are forced to do without is care, assistance with children and the elderly, the main cause being the growing feminisation of migrant labour. Women migrants supplying services as home helps or care workers in Western countries or the richest Asian countries leave not only an economic and social vacuum, but also an emotional one. It is usually other women in the family unit who replace them, since from a cultural point of view men still do not seem ready to deal with a more equal division of family management. As various research shows, the results of this phenomenon in many cases are evident in the children, the so-called 'social orphans',[26] who suffer psychologically and have behavioural problems. More and more governments are therefore imposing limits and restrictions, such as Sri Lanka, for example, which has banned mothers with children under the age of five from leaving the country. As Barbara Erhenreich rightly noted,[27] imbalances linked to the international division of care work arise, to a large extent, from the incapacity of the richest states to offer tools allowing professional and family life to be reconciled. The issue of women coming into the world of work in many industrialised countries has not caused a more equal division of care work between men and women, but the masculinisation of women in time and lifestyle. In this case migration also helps to highlight all the contradictions and dysfunctions of the richest countries and societies.

The international political vacuum

The possibility of governance of the migration processes foreseen by various analysts assumes a strong framework of regulations, a set of clear, shared rules between states, with the consent of the societies of destination. The legal tools to protect economic migrants, those at the top of the UN system, have been in place for decades, but have hardly been applied until now. The problem does not seem to be one of writing new rules, but of having the existing ones ratified and complied with.

This is particularly true of the international Convention on the Protection of the Rights of All Migrant Workers and Members of Their Families,[28] adopted at the UN General Meeting on 18 December 1990, the same date that was then chosen as World Migrant Day. It is without doubt the most complete international treaty in terms of human rights for economic migrants and is aimed at providing a universal standard of protection for both documented and undocumented immigrants, both on the labour market and in social life and access to services. In fact the Convention – which came into force on the 20th ratification in 2003 – did not introduce new rights, but provided protection against abuse and discrimination all along the migration route, from the recruitment process until admission to the foreign country. Made up of 93 articles and nine parts, the Convention includes some substantial rights that regulate and provide access to information on working conditions, taking part in trade union organisations, equality of treatment compared with local workers, transfer of remittances and family reunions, for example. Protection obligations are also provided not only for the countries of destination, but also the countries of origin. These include providing correct information on the regulations for admission and conditions of work abroad, setting up assistance and monitoring of recruitment agencies, making return routes easier and allowing denouncement of illegal practices and recourse to the law. They are rules designed with situations in mind where the lack of general shared references leaves the life of workers open to the possibility of bilateral and discretionary agreements by the states of both destination and origin, which are just as responsible for the violations of rights suffered by their citizens.

There is therefore a supranational legal reference system aimed at preventing abuse that would allow a first step towards global governance; it is only governments undertaking to abide by its provisions that are lacking. Up to September 2012 only 46 states had ratified the Convention.[29] These did not include the countries of destination, the rich countries – and not one was from the EU. Ban Ki-Moon, UN General Secretary, called it a really 'disappointing' result in a speech to the Council of Europe: 'Twenty years after it was adopted, none of Europe's largest and most wealthy powers have signed or ratified it. In some of the world's most advanced democracies among nations that take just pride in their long history of social progressiveness migrants are being denied their basic human rights.'[30]

And yet throughout the process of drafting the treaty, which lasted about 20 years, a decisive role was played by EU member states. According to Graziano Battistella,[31] an international migration scholar, the text of the Convention is fundamentally a European text. For this reason the decision not to ratify it by leading countries in matters of human rights has caused surprise and disappointment in the international community. In spite of major campaigns by NGOs and a large part of civil society, EU countries decided to concentrate on the aspect of admission and control of borders rather than respecting the human rights of anyone within the EU, taking no account of their legal or illegal status, as the Convention would have imposed. This political decision produced a discouraging effect in terms of support and ratification in all areas where Western Europe has a strong influence, such as North Africa and Central Eastern Europe. Today the EU and the international community do not know what to do with this Convention. In analysing the story of this treaty, researchers Paul de Guchteneire and Antoine Pécoud[32] put forward three main theories: abandon the text and let all the work done so far go for nothing, or try and find an alternative version, perhaps more limited and less binding, or return to promoting it in the hope that the need to regulate international migration, which is felt even more today, will drive people to look for a reference system to unify policies and practice.

No to the trade unions

One of the reasons why the Convention was produced in 1990 was the desire to surpass existing conventions relating to migrant work, of which in essence there were two, both produced by the ILO. The most recent, Convention No 143, on discrimination against legal and illegal migrants, dates back to 1975. Then, two well-known countries of origin, Mexico and Morocco, started a campaign to draw up a new treaty. Böhning[33] suggests that they did so because they were against relying on the ILO to regulate a matter of such strategic importance for their economies. This UN agency, the ILO, it must be recalled, is the only one with a tripartite structure, made up in equal measure of representatives of governments, companies and trade unions. The fear that the trade unions would have a binding role led these governments to look for an alternative. Also, unlike the ILO conventions, those of the UN could be ratified with reservations, therefore presenting a greater degree of flexibility. These elements confirm the theory that in reality governments continue to reject a system of regulation that is really shared and binding. They also confirm the advance of a strong anti-trade union culture with the view that migrant work must be more and more subject to market forces and not the force of law. The contents of the 1990 Convention had already been widely anticipated by two ILO regulations, Nos 97 and 143.[34] The ILO conventions set international standards for work, covering every single aspect of the working life of people. The texts are drawn up and adopted by the ILO through the tripartite system, therefore with full participation by governments, companies and trade unions from the 185 member states, to then be ratified by individual governments, who in this way undertake to accept their contents and translate them into ordinary laws. From that moment the ILO provides constant monitoring of application of the conventions, which have been ratified, and indicates any violations through its commissions.

The 1949 Convention on Migration for Work, No 97, was ratified by 49 countries, while the 1975 Convention on Migrant Workers, No 143, obtained 23 ratifications. In Europe, Convention No 97 was accepted by a large proportion of the first 15 states of the EU, while only Italy and Portugal adopted Convention No 143. Neither have been ratified by the countries receiving the most migrants in the world, which are, in order: the US, Russian Federation, Germany (which ratified Convention No 97) and Saudi Arabia. Both conventions refer to workers who are employed, not independent, and protect them throughout the whole migration process: emigration, transit and immigration. They concern both seasonal and permanent migrants and include refugees and displaced people if they are involved in work activity. The regulations do not cover any specific categories of workers, such as seamen and border guards, for example, or students carrying out training apprenticeships.

Convention No 143, was adopted in the 1970s, a period when high levels of unemployment and illegal immigration were driving governments to control and regulate flows, as seen regarding the situation in the US and France (see Chapters 2 and 3). It was the result of the first multilateral attempt to deal with the problem of legal and illegal migration with the specific aim of hitting traffickers and those employers who discriminated against and penalised immigrants compared with locals, particularly those found without documents and who were victims of abuse. In 1998 the ILO Commission of Experts highlighted the need to update the regulations in view of the most recent changes in migration, such as movements becoming shorter, the feminisation of migrant work, the decreasing effect of national policies on economic processes and the spread of private agencies acting as middlemen, for example. The two conventions have also so far not managed to impose the production of a national immigration policy on the governments that ratified them. According to the tripartite nature of the ILO, this must involve representatives of employers and of workers as well as government.

In 2004 the ILO started work on a 'multilateral framework for migration for work'[35] during the 92nd International Labour Conference. From the first discussions on the need to define parameters for the conditions of migrant workers in the global economy, the ILO drew up a list of non-binding principles for an approach to managing immigration based on fundamental rights, the principles of 'decent work' and proper policies for integration and social inclusion. In 2006 the ILO governing body approved the distribution of these guidelines[36] in all member countries to draw attention to compliance with Convention Nos 97 and 143 and relevant recommendations as reference points not only for protecting the rights of migrant workers, but also as an introduction to the wider question of migration and development. It is significant that in the subtitle of the publication of the *Multilateral framework*, 'the absence of obligations' is specified, almost as though it were about advice and good practice to be followed, and not binding rules for member states. This fear of imposing the least regulation shows the weakness of UN agencies faced with the possibility of creating any form of global governance of the phenomenon of migration. Therefore the governments of the countries of destination and for different reasons those of the countries of origin are continuing to avoid any supranational control. This resistance is only prolonging the political vacuum where movements of people take place and they continue to bear the whole weight of migration, with all its contradictions and imbalances.

Where is Europe?

At the end of 2011 the European Parliament approved the Single Permit Directive,[37] which ratifies equality of rights between migrant and EC workers. The intention is to give official recognition to titles and qualifications, taxation and professional training, access to social security and unemployment benefit and the transferability of pensions accumulated. The Directive has been presented as a decisive step forward in a more realistic and economically more efficient migration policy. 'It is evident that labour migration will be a part of all our societies in the future,'[38] said Commissioner for Internal Affairs Cecilia Malmström. According to the Commissioner, 'to ensure prosperity, Europe must become a more attractive destination in the global competition for talent'.

Member states have been given two years to translate the new measures into national laws, which do not affect the possibilities governments have of regulating the flow of non-EU workers, but only oblige them to respond to a request for a single permit within a time limit of four months. The 2011 Directive is an addition to the one in 2009 that set up the blue card[39] following the example of the

US green card, and will speed up the procedure for issuing a special permit to stay and work for more qualified foreigners. Therefore the administrative procedure for legal admission in individual countries continues to be improved but is still far from the idea of supranational cooperation and an immigration policy that takes international political and economic relationships into account,[40] especially as there are still some countries (the UK, Denmark and Ireland) that have chosen not to apply the two Directives.

The EU is proceeding uncertainly, trying to mediate between market forces that want to open borders to the free supply of foreign labour, and internal political pressures that instead tend to close borders, worrying about keeping and providing rights and services, particularly for citizens and local workers. And yet the long process of setting up the EU has been accompanied by attempts to harmonise migration policies and to regulate the mobility of labour realistically. The free circulation of community workers was already provided when the Common Market was set up in the Treaty of Rome in 1957. The idea was to produce an internal market that would allow the circulation of goods, services, people and capital within an economic system based on cohesion and harmonisation of regulations. Still, besides monetary and economic union, the Maastricht Treaty in 1992 established European citizenship with the first definition of the internal borders of the EU that were to be removed. Community migration policy was determined partly by supranational procedures, attributing major powers to the EU, and partly by justice and internal affairs, leaving a wider decision-making margin to individual states instead.

With the subsequent Amsterdam Treaty in 1997 most EU countries complied with the Schengen Agreement, which abolished controls on people at the internal borders of the European area and reinforced controls at the external borders. This treaty transferred a large number of the questions linked to migration, such as the right to asylum, the system of entry visas, the regulation of external borders and repatriation practices, to community responsibility. The highest level of harmonisation was only reached in regulating asylum with the Dublin Convention from 1990, which gave the first member state the responsibility of examining and responding to the request for asylum. This Convention caused an understandable movement of asylum-seekers towards countries granting protection more easily, such as those of Northern Europe, crossing Mediterranean countries illegally and running thousands of risks, as shown in Chapter 3, with the many stories of young Iraqis and Afghanis at the port of Calais, in France, for example.

The European Council of Tampere in 1999 showed the need for convergence between the various national legislations relating to non-community workers and citizens being admitted and staying. This special Council marked an important stage in trying to harmonise these policies, considering the economic and demographic situation of both the EU countries and the countries of origin. The aim, formally at least, was to encourage legal immigration and to stop immigration without documents by working with the countries of origin and transit, and generally following the principle of equal, non-discriminatory treatment of migrants, providing the possibility of political and social as well as economic inclusion for this reason. In theory the Tampere strategy also included cooperation in development, a decisive element for limiting expulsion factors from the poorest countries.[41] The principles of inclusion and equality of treatment were then included in the Charter of Fundamental Rights of the EU (the Nice Charter) in 2000. Following this the EU Commission suggested to the member states that they connect the permit to stay with the work contract according to the usual guest worker model, aiming to encourage bureaucratic simplification and harmonise regulations to remove inequalities in treatment. In the same year, the Lisbon Strategy reformulated community economic policies, more and more directed towards competition. Based on this Strategy, 'immigration for economic reasons must respond to a common assessment of the needs of the labour markets in the EU'.[42] This market culture determined employment policies not only for migrants but also for EU citizens. It was a question of a major reappraisal of the culture affirmed by 20th-century Constitutions in many European countries, based on the principle of work as a right. This principle had imposed economic policies on states to increase employment, encourage growth and provide social cohesion.[43] The Lisbon Strategy formally set the objective of full employment, but the policies that followed over the last few years – directed towards labour flexibility – and the clear predominance of market arguments over labour and social arguments gave the lie to the initial rhetoric. As far as migrant work was concerned, a 'Green Paper' on the approach of the EU to the management of economic migration[44] was presented by the European Commission in 2005, due to a declared 'urgent need for a new work force in view of a continuously ageing population and market demand'. The matter of irregular migration and subsequent exploitation was still considered in mere terms of security, however. With the growing perception of international insecurity fuelled by post-September 11 terrorist incidents and new wars in the Middle East, the initial idea of an open and multilateral European migration policy was replaced progressively by a closed, security-based, defensive approach. A special agency was dedicated to the 'integrated management of external borders', Frontex, as a tool for stopping illegal immigration, which also discourages entry by asylum-seekers and victims of trafficking, who should have every right to protection instead. Controls have been concentrated predominantly on the outside and are aimed at monitoring the borders and punishing illegal immigrants rather than acting against the exploitation of labour within individual countries.[45]

Refugees of the economic crisis

The 2008 financial crisis increased difficulties with economic migration. It had an immediate impact on admission policies, restricting permits to stay and limiting visas to the duration of the work contract. Most of the 27 countries of the EU have reduced admission quotas for work and family reunion, some have increased deportations of those without valid documents and have created voluntary repatriation systems through pay-to-go incentives, even after years of living in Europe.[46]

Migrant workers have undoubtedly been the worst hit by the crisis. According to a study by IOM,[47] while the unemployment rate for European citizens increased by 2.8 per cent between 2008 and 2009, the rate for extra-European citizens went up by 5 per cent, a difference due to some extent to the high concentration of non-community workers in the building, distribution, tourism and catering sectors, which have been the worst affected by the recession. There has been less of an impact on women, particularly those working in care services, which are on the increase throughout Western Europe. The IOM reports that migrants are reluctant to claim benefits and allowances, even though they are more exposed to unemployment. It is also highly likely that the numbers of illegal immigrants have increased because, after they have been dismissed, many are unable to find new employment within the validity period of their visa and remain after it has expired.

During the crisis various scholars warned that you could not just close the borders and send immigrants back to the poorest countries, to which development funds were being cut. Long before the Arab revolts and revolutions the political analyst Arno Tanner observed that in Africa growing poverty, together with the food and health crisis, was already increasing social conflicts with the resulting repression by authoritarian regimes. In the case of Egypt in 2009 the government of Hosni Mubarak had sent in the police with truncheons and tear gas to stop demonstrations against the increase in the price of flour and to prevent attacks on granaries. More and more young people were forced to flee and seek not just work, but also protection. Tanner then proposed extending the status of refugee not only to those fleeing from wars, persecution or natural disasters, but also those fleeing the many repercussions of the economic recession.

'The world financial crisis will weaken African economic growth and food provision. A mixture of rising food prices, increasing difficulty to secure international loans, deteriorating export avenues, and shrinking labour markets will cause brain drain, societal unrest, and conflict. Unrest and conflict will exacerbate human rights problems and refugee flows, another kind of migration,' Tanner wrote in March 2009 in *The Harvard International Review*.[48] We would soon have seen those migrants, whom Tanner had described as refugees of the economic crisis and whom Europe should have treated differently, granting them the same protection as reserved for victims of humanitarian crises. In short, European reception programmes should be reconsidered and extended to prepare for the possibility of crises in migration from Africa, providing at least temporary protection.

The economic crisis should also not force cuts to be made in aid and funds intended for international cooperation because this will produce even greater migratory flows in the long term.

On the day after the Arab Spring EU leaders tried to show their willingness to help the North African region, announcing aid and reform projects aimed at providing greater stability and development, but above all preventing further exoduses. In the first few months of 2011 the High Representative of the EU for Foreign Affairs and Security Policy, Catherine Ashton, allocated funds and organised a series of international conferences on building democracy in the countries of North Africa, based, she said, on respect for human rights. This was 'belated activism', wrote the *Libération* daily,[49] because the EU had been limited to 'registering the fall of "friendly" dictatorships, incapable of taking even the slightest initiative'. Even at the height of the emergency, when in the month of February 2011 alone more than 6,000 Tunisians arrived on the Italian island of Lampedusa over two weeks, Commissioner Malmström limited herself to sending a mission from the Frontex agency 'as a sign of European solidarity'.[50] This is the same Commissioner who a few months earlier had signed an agreement with Gaddafi to patrol the borders of southern Libya and therefore push African migrants and refugees even further away from Europe. The Frontex mission, a small group of officials who were in Lampedusa for a few days, served little purpose, since the burden of receiving people fleeing from the riots in North Africa fell on neighbouring countries, and on Italy to a much smaller extent. For some weeks the Italian and French authorities offloaded onto each other the responsibility for about 20,000 Tunisians who had crossed the Mediterranean, climbed up the boot of Italy and tried to cross the border to enter France. In this case too the EU made no pronouncement, it could not produce a strategy or find a common political line to help manage the situation. There simply wasn't any.

The potential of the diaspora

'Immigrant networks are a rare bright spark in the world economy.' This is the subtitle of a long special issue *The Economist* dedicated to contemporary migration.[51] The title was 'The magic of diasporas' and it was inspired by the idea that the mobility of labour increases opportunities for development in the countries of origin and enriches the countries of destination.

This British weekly, the authoritative voice of Western capitalism, adopted an unexpectedly critical position on the subject of clichés regarding migrants, who are often described as parasites taking resources away from welfare in rich countries or jobs away from locals. 'Migrants tend to be hard-working and innovative,' it says, 'which spurs productivity and company formation.' The interest of *The Economist* is in showing the potential for innovation and development that is inherent in the migration process. This view comes from the historical fact that migration networks have always generated powerful economic forces, as maintained by Georg Simmel and Werner Sombart at the beginning of the 20th century in their analysis of modern capitalism. According to these two economists, migration necessarily involves change because it arises out of a selection from the most determined and most enterprising, those ready to rethink existing social relationships. The reference was above all to traders, particularly Jewish ones, who had broken away from local community ties and were moving dynamically in the international context of the time, encouraging commercialism and therefore the accumulation of capital. 'For the emigrant ... there is no past and no present, there is only the future,' wrote Sombart.[52]

The greater ease of movement and communication that exists today has increased this potential and made networks wider and more numerous. Diasporas spread work, information and knowledge because many are trained in Western countries and then return home, applying what they have learned outside, according to the theory of social remittances. Diasporas also spread money through economic remittances and through better circulation of transnational investments. A study by Duke University shows that, although they represent only an eighth of the US population, immigrants founded a quarter of the technology and engineering companies of the US.[53] Creating connections with emerging markets, migration also helps industrialised countries to become part of the economies that are growing most quickly, those that until now only exported their labour force, like the so-called 'BRICS', namely Brazil, Russia, India, China and South Africa.

Although this is true for high-tech and strategic sectors, it is worth considering that in many countries of destination, characterised by small and medium-sized companies in traditional sectors, the activities of immigrants are in a weak, marginal position, and larger companies often offload the risks and costs of subcontracting services that are low intensive in capital and high intensive in unqualified labour onto them. If instead networks of foreign companies were included and made the most of the economies of small industrial districts due to their specific nature, they could play a decisive, innovative role, directed towards new markets and exploiting transnational links, for which immigrants already have the social capital. The real potential lies in the possibility of offering support to the production and reproduction of a new entrepreneurial manufacturing class, restructuring local work culture.[54]

The digital community

The Economist has got it right, however, regarding the potential arising from the relationship between migration and technology. Well-known research by the University of Cambridge,[55] with the prophetic title 'The digital diaspora', highlights how the new information and communication tools that are available are helping to modify mobility from a social, cultural and political point of view. It is more and more difficult for migration to be reduced to a movement between two different communities belonging to completely separate places, characterised by independent systems of social relationships, as previously happened.[56] On the contrary, more and more migrants maintain relationships at a distance in the forms typical of close relationships, constantly building bridges and making connections. This culture of links has become much more dynamic since those who are moving systematically use information and communication technology tools. Scholars maintain that at the same time, technology allows 'rooting', strengthening the link with their origin and increasing their knowledge of it, and 'routing' contacts, distributing communication and relationships with various people, friends and family within a transnational network system.[57] This is a double action, making the relationship even more fluid and dynamic with two or more communities, of which they have physically or virtually become a part, with places and cultures crossed by migrants who increasingly take no account of the geographical dimension.

For the purposes of social and political inclusion the most important difference is the greater level of involvement of technology. The protagonists of diasporas are very active in online discussions generated by information channels, real cultural intermediaries of today, particularly when dealing with identity and nationality.[58] They do this through social networks, like blogs, creating new types of social-political space and reaffirming feelings of transnational solidarity. In the 'digital public sphere' the new media may increase participatory and democratic potential, allowing a level of access to information and knowledge in ways that were previously completely unthinkable.

Therefore the role of technology also leads to traditional categories of migration being rethought and their current social significance being understood. There is a nationalist and ethnocentric view in which governments continue to regard migration as something temporary to be suffered, contained and stopped, rather than a physiological phenomenon of the mobility of people, the natural product of the new international division of labour. Migration needs to be 'de-exceptionalised', suggests Andrea Mubi Brighenti,[59] because it is not a specific, separate element within society but an integral part of a wider system. Brighenti invokes the need for a 'new sociology of borders', aimed at showing that these are no longer just geographical lines, they are not only on the borders of states, but are much more widespread and have infiltrated into the social, cultural and legal fields that really determine the inclusion and exclusion of individuals.

The result is non-linear mobility, which happens through various spheres of economic and social organisation, rather than through the states. The example of the digital diaspora is useful in showing how the frontier of knowledge, for instance, needs to be redefined. There is more and more distance in terms of access to knowledge between digital natives and digital migrants, respectively, those who belong to the 'net generation',[60] born in the 1990s, and previous generations.

And this kind of frontier corresponds less and less to geographical borders. You need only think of the young bloggers who triggered the Arab Spring and then physically moved to Europe. Do they not represent an example of digital natives, born, living and moving freely within the network environment? And yet for the geography of the states, they are only potential migrants, often undocumented or 'clandestine'.

This is the direction taken by the reflection in *The Economist* on the potential of diasporas due to the innovative capacity of migrants, a capacity, however, which does not necessarily have to refer to development as understood economically, to business, because above all the migrant is an innovator of cultural, social and political life, a person maintaining complex relationships in both a structural and spatial sense, as sociologists tend to say. Following the idea that transmigrants move in an increasingly fluid way in relationships between capital and work, Saskia Sassen notes that global capital and the new immigrant labour force are two basic examples of categories/transnational players with transnational unifying capacity in a relationship where they challenge each other.[61]

This relationship of challenge and conflict is the basis for the theory of the immigrant war. The unifying capacity of the immigrant labour force today could contribute decisively to social and trade union fights being reorganised politically and a collective will being formed to oppose the excessive biopower of capital. Network relationships created by transmigrants and encouraged by technological infrastructure are effective for producing a response by organised labour with reference to the general attack by capital, which produces insecurity, exploitation and social insecurity almost everywhere. The stories in the first four chapters all show the potential for a new conflict and for the restoration of rights, of social justice and democracy. Whether it is the struggles of Asian workers in the building sites of Dubai, of the Mexican farm labourers in the fields of California, of the undocumented African cooks in the restaurants of Paris or of the Moroccan metalworkers in Italian factories, the migrant fights are more and more determined to bring labour back to the centre of contemporary societies.

Work and citizenship

The idea of a transnational resistance of migrants cannot leave aside the elements of inclusion, citizenship and the relationship this has to work. From the examples given in the preceding chapters it has been seen how legislation in various countries is gradually hardening towards naturalisation and granting citizenship[62] with the reaffirmation of *jus sanguinis*, which is linked to descent, even in systems based on the opposite principle of *jus soli*, as in France and the US. Among theoreticians opposing this policy of closure, Linda Bosniak insists on the possibility of and opportunity for the 'denationalisation of citizenship' developing in a transnational sense, like other economic and political institutions, which have been transformed by the globalisation process as a result of the erosion of the borders of the nation-state.[63]

The greatest obligations that states today place on granting citizenship have considerable social implications that do not follow a realistic approach. Inclusion is effective with reference to both the democratic rights, on which Western systems are based, and the prevention of exclusion, which represents a clear threat to social cohesion and a reason for social trouble and deviance. This is particularly true for descendants of immigrants, who say they are dissatisfied due to difficulties with citizenship and because they often suffer from stigmatisation and discrimination.[64] Both in the US, as Alejandro Portes observed, and in Europe, second generations often live 'trapped' between two societies: the host society that does not accept them completely and the society of origin that they no longer feel part of. In 2000 the European Council asked member states to extend political participation progressively to immigrants through the right to vote and also the possibility of being a candidate in local and regional elections. The European Parliament did the same, but even today this access to non-Community citizens has been blocked in various ways by a series of restrictions.[65]

With citizenship highly subject to conditions and without the right to vote, the possibilities of inclusion for a migrant are all concentrated in the dimension of work. On the citizenship route traditionally followed by local citizens, according to the well-known definition by Thomas Marshall,[66] they go from civil rights to political rights to social rights, therefore to the right to work. Migrants instead find themselves following the completely reverse route because through work (legal) they obtain some social rights, of which the rights to healthcare, education and a home also form a part. The decision by governments to grant social rights is not motivated by ethical principles so much as by the need to harmonise the conditions of immigrant workers and those of locals, and therefore prevent competition bringing down labour costs. But social rights are not then followed by political rights, which are understood as taking part in exercising power, at least through the vote.

This causes a situation where foreigners are without doubt weaker and more difficult to protect and immigration is perceived as a phenomenon that is still temporary and transitory. In short, this confirms the logic of being exclusively functional with reference to the needs of the market. As Sassen[67] puts it, unlike the citizen, the immigrant is constructed in law and through policy as a partial subject, while immigration and immigrants are 'solid realities'. There emerges the evident contradiction of nation-state belonging and the inner tension of today's market-driven economies. Therefore, in reversing the classic route indicated by Marshall, these social rights, which have been determined by work, could now be considered elements constituting a new idea of social citizenship, regarding which any reference to nationality is and must remain extraneous.[68] In other words, work and associated rights must represent the essential condition for immigrants to then proceed to full citizenship. Through immigration today it is possible to verify the potential of the right to work, which increasingly constitutes an important factor for promoting citizenship and a tool for integrating the excluded. In this sense work could reactivate the historical function of a tool for the material organisation of society, forming the basis for citizenship.

Notes

Chapter 1

[1] BK stands for Bishworkarma, categorised as Dalits and who were once treated as 'untouchables'; they fall in the lowest rung of caste hierarchy.

[2] Parashar, U. (2011) 'Dreams ending in wooden coffins', Blogs, Kurakani in Kathmandu, *Hindustan Times* online, 20 April (http://blogs.hindustantimes.com/kurakani-in-kathmandu/2011/04/20/dreams-ending-in-wooden-coffins/).

[3] Adhikari, D. (2010) 'A casket of dreams: deaths of Nepali migrants overseas', *Kathmandu Post*, 20 February (www.ekantipur.com/2010/02/20/oped/a-casket-of-dreams/308742/).

[4] Pattinson, P. (Director) (2010) *The cost of living* (Documentary), International Trade Union Confederation (ITUC), Anti-Slavery International.

[5] ITUC (International Trade Union Confederation) (2012) 'New evidence of abuses of workers' rights in Qatar prompts ITUC investigation', Press release, 16 May.

[6] Sedhai, R. (2012) '3,000 Nepalis die in Saudi in 12 yrs', *The Kathmandu Post* online, 1 July (www.ekantipur.com/the-kathmandu-post/2012/07/01/top-story/3000-nepalis-die-in-saudi-in-12-yrs/236655.html).

[7] Interview, 13 December 2011.

[8] Adhikari, op cit.

[9] World Bank (2011) *The migration and remittances factbook*, Washington, DC: The World Bank.

[10] http://siteresources.worldbank.org/INTPROSPECTS/Resources/334934-1110315015165/MigrationandDevelopmentBrief18.pdf

[11] Erhenreich, B. (2004) *Donne globali* [*Global women*], Milan: Feltrinelli.

[12] BBC News (2010) 'Maid "tortured" with nails to have surgery', BBC News online, 26 August (www.bbc.co.uk/news/world-south-asia-11094968).

[13] Jayaruk, K.J. (2010) 'I have no reason to lie: Ariyawathie', *Sunday Times* online, 5 September (http://sundaytimes.lk/100905/News/nws_47.html).

[14] World Bank (2010) Development Prospects Group; UNPD (2009).

[15] World Bank (2011), op cit.

[16] BBC News (2008) 'Saudi maid verdict "outrageous"', BBC News online, 22 May (http://news.bbc.co.uk/2/hi/7415290.stm).

[17] de Parle, J. (2011) 'Domestic workers convention may be landmark', *The New York Times* online, 8 October (www.nytimes.com/2011/10/09/world/domestic-workers-convention-may-be-landmark.html).

[18] David, N. (2010) *From Bahrain to Malaysia: Mobilising to defend migrants' rights*, Union View, International Trade Union Confederation.

[19] UN News Centre (2010) '"Encouraging" changes under way in Persian Gulf countries, says UN rights chief', UN News Centre, 19 April (www.un.org/apps/news/story.asp?NewsID=34404&Cr=Pillay&Cr1).

[20] See www.gcc-sg.org/eng/index.html

[21] Ambrosetti, E. and Tattolo, G. (2004) *Pétrole et migrations de travail vers les pays du Golfe* [*Oil and work migration to the Gulf States*], Paris: Actes du Colloques de Budapest, pp 355-66.

[22] Colton, N.A. (2011) 'The international political economy of Gulf migration', in *Migration and the Gulf: Viewpoints*, Washington DC: Middle East Institute.

[23] Kanna, A. (2011) 'The Arab world's forgotten rebellions: foreign workers and biopolitics in the Gulf', *Samar: South Asian Magazine for Action and Reflection*, 31 May.

[24] The expression usually refers to those states that are rich in highly valued natural resources such as oil and may generate rents, therefore not requiring a strong domestic productive sector.

[25] Winkler, O. (2011) 'Labour migration in the GCC states: patterns, scale, and politics', in *Migration and the Gulf: Viewpoints*, Washington DC: Middle East Institute, p 10.

[26] Kanna, op cit.

[27] David, op cit.

[28] ITUC (International Trade Union Confederation) (2011) 'Migrant worker misery lies behind gleaming towers of Gulf cities', in *Hidden faces of the Gulf miracle*, Union View.

[29] ITUC (International Trade Union Confederation) (2011) 'Amid Gulf riches migrants forced to live in squalid slums', in *Hidden faces of the Gulf miracle*, Union View.

[30] Roper, S.D. (2008) *Labor migration to the Gulf: Understanding variations in the kafala system*, Charleston, IL: Eastern Illinois University.

[31] US Department of State (2009) *Human rights report: Qatar*, Washington, DC.

[32] ILO (International Labour Organization) Regional Office for Arab States (2011) *Regional overview*, January, Geneva.

[33] Interview, 8 December 2011.

[34] ILO (International Labour Organization), ILOLEX, Database of international labour standards (www.ilo.org/ilolex/english/index.htm).

[35] ITUC (International Trade Union Confederation) (2011) *Annual survey of violations of trade union rights*, Brussels.

[36] Bristol Rhys, J. (2011) 'A lexicon of migrants in the United Arab Emirates', in *Migration and the Gulf*, Middle East Institute Viewpoints, p 2.

[37] Gardner, A. (2011) 'Labour camps in the Gulf States', in *Migration and the Gulf: Viewpoints*, Washington DC: Middle East Institute, p 55.

[38] Real News Network, The (2011) 'Migrant workers in the Gulf: a historical perspective' (video), 16 May.

[39] Interview, 8 December 2011.

[40] David, N. (2010) 'We do not differentiate between locals and migrants', in *From Bahrain to Malaysia: Mobilising to defend migrants' rights*, Union View: International Trade Union Confederation.

[41] Interview, 8 December 2011.

[42] BICI (Bahrain Independent Commission of Inquiry) (2011) *Report of the Bahrain Independent Commission of Inquiry*, 23 November.

[43] BICI, op cit.

[44] ITUC (International Trade Union Confederation) (2011) 'Bahrain: exploitation of migrant workers, including for political reasons, puts their lives at risk', 1 April, cross-posted from ITUC online (www.solidaritycenter.org/content.asp?contentid=1184).

[45] Interview, 8 December 2011.

[46] Interview, 5 December 2011.

[47] CEC (Centre for Education and Communication) and MFA (Migrant Forum in Asia) (2009) *India: Towards a holistic international migration policy*, Delhi: CEC, May, p 9.

[48] On 18 December 1990 the UN General Assembly adopted the International Convention on the Protection of the Rights of All Migrant Workers and Members of Their Families, within the scope of integrating the existing regulations promoted by ILO Convention No 97 of 1949 and No 143 of 1975.

[49] Grumiau, S. (2010) 'In Nepal, GEFONT is taking preventative action', in *From Bahrain to Malaysia: Mobilising to defend migrants' rights*, Union View, International Trade Union Confederation.

[50] Pattinson, op cit.

[51] ITUC (International Trade Union Confederation) (2012) 'Kuwait and Bahrain become first Gulf countries to forge an official trade union relationship with Nepal', Press release, 16 January.

[52] Burj Khalifa (2011) 'Stay with Armani' (www.burjkhalifa.ae/armani-hotel.aspx).

[53] Zawya (2008) 'Burj Dubai offices to top US$4,000 per sq ft', 5 March (www.zawya.com/story.cfm/sidZAWYA20080305042540?pass=1).

[54] Bedell, G. (2010) 'Burj Khalifa – a bleak symbol of Dubai's era of bling', *The Observer*, 10 January.

[55] Lloyd Wright, F. (2004) *Architettura e democrazia* (original title *Modern architecture*), Conferences held at the University of Princeton in 1930, Rome: Mancosu Editore.

[56] Bedell, op cit.

[57] Reuters (2011) 'Suicides shed light on darker side of Dubai's glitz', 2 June.

[58] Murphy, B. (2011) 'Dubai plans to deport striking Asian workers', Arabnews.com, 26 January (www.arabnews.com/node/366483).

[59] Porimol, P. (2011) 'UAE deports 71 Bangladeshi workers', *The Daily Star* online, 2 February (www.thedailystar.net/newDesign/news-details.php?nid=172541).

[60] Kanna, op cit.

[61] ILO (International Labour Organization) Beirut (2004) *Gender and migration in the Arab States, the case of domestic workers*, Geneva.

[62] Corpuz, N. (2010) *Filipino domestic workers: The struggle for justice and survival*, Geneva: ITC-ILO.

[63] See http://migranteinternational.org/

[64] Jara-Puyod, M. (2011) 'Anti-trafficking council: Philippines' BI needs to explain offloading policy', *The Gulf Today* online, 18 October (http://gulftoday.ae/portal/63663386-b80b-4a62-93fa-97baf595240b.aspx).

[65] Ponce de Leon, J. (2011) 'Manila to set guidelines for immigration bureau's role', Gulfnews.com, 30 October (http://gulfnews.com/news/gulf/uae/visa/manila-to-set-guidelines-for-immigration-bureau-s-role-1.920375).

[66] Kanna, op cit.

[67] ITUC (International Trade Union Confederation) (2010) 'Middle East: a nightmare for all too many domestic workers', in *From Bahrain to Malaysia: Mobilising to defend migrants' rights*, Union View: ITUC.

[68] Human Rights Watch (2011) 'Jordan: domestic worker protections ineffective', 27 September, *News* (www.hrw.org/news/2011/09/27/jordan-domestic-worker-protections-ineffective).

[69] ILO (International Labour Organization) (2011) '100th ILO annual conference decides to bring an estimated 53 to 100 million domestic workers worldwide under the realm of labour standards', 16 June, *Media Centre* (www.ilo.org/ilc/ILCSessions/100thSession/media-centre/press-releases/WCMS_157891/lang--en/index.htm).

[70] ITUC (International Trade Union Confederation) (2011) 'New international convention on domestic workers' rights must be respected by governments, says global union body', ITUC online, 16 June.

[71] The '12 by 12' campaign was an initiative of the International Trade Union Confederation (ITUC) and of the International Domestic Workers Network (IDWN), the European Trade Union Confederation (ETUC), Public Service International (PSI), the International Union of Food, Agricultural, Hotel, Restaurant, Catering, Tobacco and Allied Workers' Associations (IUF), Human Rights Watch, Anti-Slavery International, Solidar, Migrant Forum Asia (MFA), World Solidarity and Caritas.

[72] ITUC (International Trade Union Confederation) (2012) 'Keep up pressure on governments for the ratification of the Domestic Workers Convention', ITUC online, 16 June.

Chapter 2

[1] Stevenson, M. and Castillo, E. (2010) '72 bodies found dumped in Mexico', *The Huffington Post* and Associated Press, 25 August (www.huffingtonpost.com/2010/08/25/72-bodies-found-dumped-in_n_693723.html).

[2] Schepers, E. (2011) 'Mexican kidnappings reveal ongoing abuse of migrant workers', People's World online, 5 January (http://peoplesworld.org/mexican-kidnappings-reveal-ongoing-abuse-of-migrant-workers/).

[3] BBC News (2010) 'Mexico migrants face human rights crisis, says Amnesty', BBC World News online, 29 April (http://news.bbc.co.uk/2/hi/8647252.stm).

[4] World Bank (2011) *The migration and remittances factbook*, Washington, DC.

[5] (2012) 'El Congreso ordena la publicación de la Ley de Víctimas sin cambios' ['Congress ordered the publication of Victims Act unchanged'], CNN Mexico online, 11 July (http://mexico.cnn.com/nacional/2012/07/11/el-congreso-ordena-la-publicacion-de-la-ley-de-victimas-sin-cambios).

[6] See www.hermanosenelcamino.org/english.html

[7] BBC News (2011) 'UN calls for Mexico probe into migrant train abductions', BBC News online, 21 January (www.bbc.co.uk/news/world-latin-america-12248508).

[8] Hyslop, L. (2011) 'Mexico tries to prevent migrant abuse', *The Telegraph* online, 27 May (www.telegraph.co.uk/expat/expatnews/8541637/Mexico-tries-to-prevent-migrant-abuse.html).

[9] (2012) "Mexico's Peña Nieto calls for 'new debate' on the drug war", CNN online, 7 July (http://articles.cnn.com/2012-07-07/americas/world_americas_mexico-elections_1_drug-war-immigration-law-labor-reform?_s=PM:AMERICAS).

[10] Regan, M. (2010) *The death of Josseline*, Boston, MA: Beacon Press.

[11] Regan, op cit, p xxi.

[12] Regan, op cit, p xxii.

[13] US Government Accountability Office (2006) *Illegal immigration: Border-crossing deaths have doubled since 1995; Border patrol's efforts to prevent deaths have not been fully evaluated*, August.

[14] Bacon, D. (2008) *Illegal people: How globalization creates migration and criminalizes immigrants*, Boston, MA: Beacon Press, p 61.

[15] Robinson, W. and Santos, X. (2007) Extract from interview obtained in September 2007, University of Santa Barbara, California.

[16] LCLAA (Labour Council for Latin American Advancement) (2011) *Latino workers in the United States*, Washington, DC.

[17] LCLAA, op cit, p 52.

[18] Work Authorization for Non-US Citizens: Temporary Agricultural Workers (H-2A visas), Employment Law Guide of the United States Department of Labor (www.dol.gov/compliance/guide/taw.htm).

[19] Work Authorization for Non-US Citizens: Temporary Nonagricultural Workers (H-2B visas), Employment Law Guide of the United States Department of Labor (www.dol.gov/compliance/guide/tnw.htm).

[20] SPLC (Southern Poverty Law Center) (2007) *Close to slavery: Guestworker programs in the United States*, Montgomery, AL.

[21] SPLC, ibid.

[22] SPLC, ibid.

[23] Human Rights Watch (2000) *Unfair advantage: Workers' freedom of association in the United States under international human rights standards*, Ithaca, NY: ILR Press.

[24] *Hector Luna et al vs Del Monte Fresh Produce (Southeast) Inc et al*, US District Court for the Northern District of Georgia, Atlanta Division, Case No 1:06-cv-02000-JEC.

[25] SPLC, op cit.

[26] LCLAA, op cit.

[27] Kennedy, J.F. (1964) *A nation of immigrants*, New York: Harper & Row.

[28] Melotti, U. (2004) *Migrazioni internazionali, globalizzazione e culture politiche* [*International migration, globalisation and political culture*], Milan: Bruno Mondadori.

[29] Ouellette, J., Magana, L. and Palmer, R. (2008) *A day without immigrants*, San Francisco, CA: Compass Point Books.

[30] Pfaelzer, J. (2007) *Driven out: The forgotten war against Chinese Americans*, New York: Random House.

[31] Melotti, op cit, p 90.

[32] Ouellette et al, op cit, p 34.

[33] Bacon, op cit, p 51.

[34] Bacon, op cit, p 53.

[35] Buchanan, P. (2007) *Day of reckoning: How hubris, ideology, and greed are tearing America apart*, New York: Thomas Dunne Books.

[36] Robinson and Santos, op cit.

[37] LCLAA, op cit, p 51.

[38] Council on Foreign Relations (2005) *Border Protection, Antiterrorism, and Illegal Immigration Control Act of 2005*, HR 4437 (www.cfr.org/about/).

[39] Ouellette et al, op cit, p 67.

[40] Robinson and Santos, op cit.

[41] Martin, D. (2005) *Haymarket*, Chicago, IL: Spartaco Editore.

[42] Arau, S. (Director) (2004) *A day without a Mexican* (Film), Altavista.

[43] Robinson and Santos, op cit.

[44] Watanabe, T. and Mathews, J. (2006) 'Unions helped to organize "Day without immigrants"', *Los Angeles Times*, 3 May.

[45] Robinson and Santos, op cit.

[46] Bacon, op cit, p 195.

[47] In 1947 the Taft-Hartley Labor Act on trade union freedom was adopted, which limited the right to bargaining. The conservative policy of President Reagan in the 1980s subsequently contributed to the reduction in the role and power of US trade unionists.

[48] Ness, I. (2005) *Immigrants, unions and the new US market*, Philadelphia, PA: Temple University Press, p 188.

[49] Schmitt, J. (2010) *Unions and upward mobility for immigrant workers*, Washington, DC: Center for Economic and Policy Research, March.

[50] LCLAA, op cit, p 53.

[51] Arnesen, E. (2006) *Encyclopedia of US labor and working-class history*, New York: Routledge.

[52] Loach, K. (Director) (2000) *Bread and roses* (Film).

[53] Ness, op cit, p 188.

[54] Ness, op cit, p 189.

[55] Otis, J. (2012) 'American unions stand up for Latin American workers', *Global Post*, 30 April (www.globalpost.com/dispatch/news/regions/americas/colombia/120430/american-unions-stand-latin-american-workers).

[56] LCLAA, op cit, p 54.

[57] AFL-CIO (American Federation of Labor and Congress of Industrial Organizations) (2011) *Seven immigration myths and facts*, Washington, DC.

[58] Trumka, R. (2011) 'Undocumented workers need legal rights', Special to CNN, 1 July (http://articles.cnn.com/2010-07-01/opinion/trumka.immigration_1_immigration-system-global-economy-american-reality?_s=PM:OPINION).

[59] Immigralaw.com (2011) Immigration quotas (www.immigralaw.com/english/immigrationquotas.html).

[60] Monger, R. and Yankay, J. (2011) *US legal permanent residents: 2010*, Washington, DC: Department of Homeland Security Office of Immigration Statistics.

[61] US Census Bureau (2010) *State and county quick facts*, Washington, DC.

[62] Passel, J. and Cohn, D. (2011) *Unauthorized immigrant population: National and state trends, 2010*, Washington, DC: Pew Research Center.

[63] AFL-CIO, op cit.

[64] AFL-CIO, ibid.

[65] Chomsky, A. (2007) *'They take our jobs!' And 20 other myths about immigration*, Boston, MA: Beacon Press.

[66] Portes, A. (2002) 'Immigration's aftermath', *The American Prospect*, vol 13, no 7, pp 9-12.

[67] Portes, ibid.

[68] AFL-CIO and Change to Win (2011) *The Labor Movement's Framework for Comprehensive Immigration Reform* (http://fcnl.org/assets/labor_movements_framework_for_reform.pdf).

[69] Archibold, R. (2010) 'Arizona enacts stringent law on immigration', *The New York Times* online, 23 April (www.nytimes.com/2010/04/24/us/politics/24immig.html).

[70] CNN (2010) 'Legal battle looms over Arizona immigration law', 28 July (http://articles.cnn.com/2010-07-28/us/arizona.immigration.law_1_arizona-immigration-law-illegal-immigrants-arizona-state?_s=PM:US).

[71] Liptak, A. (2012) 'Blocking parts of Arizona law, justices allow its centerpiece', *New York Times* online, 25 June (www.nytimes.com/2012/06/26/us/supreme-court-rejects-part-of-arizona-immigration-law.html?_r=1).

[72] Ibid.

[73] See http://dreamact.info/

[74] Obama, B. (2010) 'Transcript of Obama's immigration speech', *The Wall Street Journal* online, 1 July (http://blogs.wsj.com/washwire/2010/07/01/transcript-of-obamas-immigration-speech/).

[75] Times Topics (2011) 'Immigration and emigration', *The New York Times* online, 29 September (http://topics.nytimes.com/top/reference/timestopics/subjects/i/immigration-and-emigration/index.html).

[76] Interview, 7 October 2010.

[77] Bacon, D. (2011) 'Will public workers and immigrants march together on May Day?', *In These Times* online, 1 May (www.inthesetimes.com/working/entry/7246/will_public_workers_and_immigrants_march_together_on_may_day/).

[78] Hall, M. (2012) 'On May Day, no borders between workers', *AFL-CIO Now*, 1 May (www.aflcio.org/Blog/Global-Action/On-May-Day-No-Borders-Between-Workers).

Chapter 3

[1] Maurice, S. (2009) 'Un migrant mort dans un camion à Calais' ['A migrant dies in a lorry at Calais'], *Libération*, 31 October.

[2] MdM (Médecins du Monde) (2011) *Les conditions de vie des migrants dans le Pas de Calais* [*Living conditions for migrants in Pas de Calais*], June.

[3] MdM, ibid.

[4] Spindler, W. (2009) 'UNHCR draws road map to help people out of Calais "jungle"', UNHCR News Stories, 17 July.

[5] Spindler, ibid.

[6] Walt, V. (2009) 'Will France's immigration crackdown solve anything?', *Time* online, 22 September (www.time.com/time/printout/0,8816,1925335,00. html).

[7] MdM, op cit.

[8] EU FRA (European Union Agency for Fundamental Rights) (2011) *Migrants in an irregular situation: Access to healthcare in 10 European Union member states*, 11 October.

[9] Carr, M. (2010) 'The war against immigrants', *New York Times*, *La Repubblica*, 8 November.

[10] Article L622-1, Aide à l'entrée et au séjour irréguliers, *Code de l'entrée et du séjour des étrangers et du droit d'asile* (www.legifrance.gouv.fr).

[11] Chastand, J.B. (2009) 'Le délit de solidarité aux sans-papiers existe-t-il?' ['Does the crime of solidarity against the undocumented exist?'], *Le Monde* online, 8 April (www.lemonde.fr/imprimer/article/2009/04/08/1178134.html).

[12] Lioret, P. (Director) (2009) *Welcome* (Film), Teodora Film.

[13] Fortress Europe (2011) 'La machine à expulser. Un webdoc sui Cie francesi' ['The deportation machine: a webdoc on French identification and expulsion centres'], 8 June (http://fortresseurope.blogspot.com/2011/06/la-machine-expulser-un-webdoc-sui-cie.html).

[14] La Cimade (2010) 'L'origine de la révolte' ['The origin of the revolution'], 27 January (www.cimade.org/minisites/mesnil2/rubriques/121-L-industrie-de-l-expulsion?page_id=2154).

[15] Foucault, M. (2011) *La strategia dell'accerchiamento* [*The encirclement strategy*], Palermo: Duepunti edizioni.

[16] Foucault, ibid, p 79.

[17] Sassen, S. (1999) *Migranti, coloni, rifugiati* [*Migrants, colonists, refugees*], Milan: Feltrinelli.

[18] Melotti, U. (2004) *Migrazioni internazionali* [*International migration*], Milan: Bruno Mondadori.

[19] Sassen, op cit.

[20] Sassen, ibid.

[21] Melotti, op cit.

[22] Insee (Institut national de la statistique et des études économiques) (2006) Exploitation principale, RP2006.

[23] Sassu, V. (2011) *Là-bas la banlieue* ['Over there is the suburb'], Milan: Bevivino Editore, pp 184-5.

[24] Sassu, ibid, p 45.

[25] Touraine, A. (1991) 'Face à l'exclusion' ['Facing exclusion'], *Esprit*, No 169, pp 7-13; 'Di fronte all'esclusione', *Iter*, No 2-3, pp 13-20.

[26] Melotti, U. (ed) (2007) *Les banlieues* [*The suburbs*], Rome: Meltemi Editore, p 45.

[27] Siméant, J. (2005) 'Le sans-papier: 1973-...' ['The undocumented: 1973-...'], in *Immigration et luttes sociales: Filiations et ruptures (1968-2003)* [*Immigration and social struggles*], vol 3, Paris: Editions Mémoire-Génériques, pp 79-81.

[28] Simone, A. (2002) *Divenire sans papiers: Sociologia dei dissensi metropolitani* [*Arriving without papers: Sociology of the metropolitan dissent*], Milan: Associazione Culturale Eterotopia.

[29] Siméant, op cit, p 88.

[30] Tripier, M. (2005) 'Syndicats et "luttes d'immigrés"' ['Unions and "the struggles of immigrants"'], in *Immigration et luttes sociales: Filiations et ruptures (1968–2003)*, vol 3, Paris: Editions Mémoire-Génériques, pp 72-9.

[31] Sayad, A. (1999) *La double absence* [*Double absence*], Paris: Seuil.

[32] Sayad, ibid, p 237.

[33] Tripier, M. (1992) 'French citizens and immigrants in the workplace: Marginality of the subject, marginality of the research?', in D. Horowitz and

G. Noiriel (eds) *Immigrants in two democracies: French and American experience*, New York: New York University Press, pp 292-301.

[34] Kessous, M. (2007) 'Raymond Chauveau, un syndicaliste en rouge et noir' ['Raymond Chauveau, a black and red trade unionist'], *Le Monde*, 12 September.

[35] In order for a non-EC worker without high qualifications to be able to obtain a permit, currently the French company wanting to take him or her on must make a request to the office for immigration, which checks the qualifications of the candidate through its offices in France, or through the consulate if he or she is resident abroad. However, the final decision is made by the prefect, who grants the permit only if the contract and working conditions are in line with national regulations and particularly if it may be shown that there are no other national workers in France available or sufficiently qualified for the same job. In reality in 2008 lists were drawn up of jobs which were open to foreign workers without the need for this requirement. In 2011 under the pretext of the employment crisis the number of 'open' professions dropped from 30 to 14. See Monkan, A. (2011) 'How to get a work permit in France', 2 November (www.village-justice.com).

[36] Interview, 15 September 2011.

[37] Karl Marx used this expression to refer to unemployed workers who were ready to take over if employed workers were sacked. Companies used this 'army' as a deterrent, if legally employed workers asked for pay increases, reducing profit margins. In book I, section VII, chapter 23.3 of *Capital* Marx explains: 'The industrial reserve army puts pressure on the army of active workers during periods of stagnation and average prosperity and curbs their demands during periods of overproduction and paroxysm.'

[38] *La Forge* (2006) 'Une grève pour la régularisation d'ouvriers sans-papiers' ['A strike for the regularisation of undocumented workers', 5 October.

[39] Essonne CGT (2006) 'Blanchisserie Modeluxe à Chilly-Mazarin, La Préfecture de l'Essonne s'engage à régulariser 18 salariés "sans papiers"' ['Modeluxe Laundries at Chilly-Mazarin: the Essonne Prefecture undertakes to regularise 18 undocumented workers'], 30 October, Press release. An update by Chauveau later amended the number to 22.

[40] 9ème Collectif des sans-papiers (2007) 'Le "système Buffalo Grill"', June (http://9emecollectif.net/Le_systeme_Buffalo_Grill).

[41] Gavoille, E. (2008) 'Les cuisiniers sans papiers de la Grande Armée veulent être régularisés' ['The undocumented kitchen workers at the Grande Armée want regularisation'], 13 February, 20minutes.fr (www.20minutes. fr/article/212759/France-Les-cuisiniers-sans-papiers-de-la-Grande-Armee-veulent-etre-regularises.php).

[42] Ministère du Travail, de l'Emploi et de la Santé (2011) Loi no 2011-672, du 16 juin, relative à l'immigration, à l'intégration et à la nationalité (www.travail-emploi-sante.gouv.fr/).

[43] EU FRA, op cit.

[44] Prieur, C. et al (2012) 'Manuel Valls: Etre de gauche, ce n'est pas régulariser tous les sans-papiers' ['Manuel Valls: Being on the left doesn't mean regularising all the undocumented'], Le Monde, 27 June.

[45] ILO (International Labour Organization) (2010) International labour migration. A rights-based approach, Geneva.

[46] Interview, 21 October 2010.

[47] Libération Maroc (2010) 'Les Français contre les dérives racistes' ['The French against racist tendencies'], 4 February.

[48] Interview with Eric Fassin, 22 February 2010, by 'Une journée sans immigres' (www.la-journee-sans-immigres.org/).

[49] Ney, C. (2007) Un pouvoir nommé désir [A power named desire], Paris: Grasset.

[50] Libération (2010) 'Cette journée peut engendrer une prise de conscience' ['This day can raise awareness'], 1 March (www.liberation.fr/societe/1201254-les-immigres-des-travailleurs-comme-les-autres).

[51] PeaceReporter (2010) 'Francia, la cacciata dei Rom' ['France, the expulsion of Roma'], 19 August (http://it.peacereporter.net/articolo/23685/Francia,+la+cacciata+dei+rom).

[52] Abtan, B. (2012) 'Roms, la France doit rompre clairement avec les positions de l'été 2010', Le Monde, 7 August.

Chapter 4

[1] Repubblica.it (2011) 'Lampedusa, barcone con 25 morti nella stiva "Gridavano per uscire, li buttavano giù"' ['Lampedusa, a barge with 25 bodies in the hold, "They screamed to get out but were thrown back down"'], 1 August (http://palermo.repubblica.it/cronaca/2011/08/01/news/immigrazione_tragedia_a_lampedusa_arriva_barcone_con_25_cadaveri_a_bordo-19861199/).

[2] Repubblica.it (2011) 'Orrore dall'autopsia sugli immigrati "Picchiati a morte e non asfissiati"' ['Horror from the autopsy on the immigrants, "beaten to death and not asphyxiated"'], 3 August (http://palermo.repubblica.it/cronaca/2011/08/03/news/immigrazione-19947623).

[3] AdnKronos (2011) 'Migranti morti asfissiati in stiva, arrestati sei scafisti' ['Migrants who died in the hold, asphyxiated, six smugglers arrested'], 5 August.

[4] Fortress Europe (2010) *Statistiche sugli sbarchi nel Mediterraneo* [*Statistics on landings in the Mediterranean*], 29 October (http://fortresseurope.blogspot.com/2009/10/statistiche-sugli-sbarchi-nel.html).

[5] The Convention relating to the status of refugees was approved in Geneva on 28 July 1951 by a special UN conference. It clearly states who may be considered a refugee and indicates the forms of legal protection, other assistance and social rights that the refugee must receive from states supporting the document (www.unhcr.it/news/dir/13/convenzione-di-ginevra.html).

[6] Human Rights Watch (2010) 'Italy: offer to shelter Eritreans detained, abused by Libya', 8 July (www.hrw.org/news/2010/07/08/italy-offer-shelter-eritreans-detained-abused-libya).

[7] Biondani, P., Gatti F. and Sasso, M. (2010) 'Milano–Asmara, armi e tangenti' ['Milan–Asmara, weapons and bribes'], *L'Espresso* online, 5 February (http://espresso.repubblica.it/dettaglio/milano-asmara-armi-e-tangenti/2120317).

[8] UNHCR (United Nations High Commissioner for Refugees) (2009) 'Riammettere in Italia le persone bisognose di protezione respinte in Libia' ['Readmitting into Italy those rejected by Libya'], 12 May, Press release (www.unhcr.it/news/dir/26/view/555/riammettere-in-italia-le-persone-bisognose-di-protezione-respinte-in-libia-55500.html).

[9] Senate of the Republic (2011) 'Hearing of the spokesperson for the UNHCR Laura Boldrini regarding the situation in Lampedusa', 1 March, in *Indagine conoscitiva sui livelli e i meccanismi di tutela dei diritti umani, vigenti in Italia e nella realtà internazionale* [*Investigation findings on the levels and mechanisms of human rights protection in Italy and the international reality*], Verbatim Report No 58, Extraordinary Commission for the Protection and Promotion of Human Rights.

[10] Longhi, V. (2011) 'Is EU serious about supporting human rights across north Africa?', *The Guardian*, 25 February (www.guardian.co.uk/global-development/poverty-matters/2011/feb/25/libya-eu-human-rights-response).

[11] Del Grande, G. (2011) 'Sbarchi: c'è un mandante ed è un uomo di Gheddafi ['The landings: there is an instigator and it's one of Gaddafi's men'], Fortress Europe (http://fortresseurope.blogspot.com/2011/05/il-mandante.html).

[12] See www.cronachediordinariorazzismo.org/il-rapporto-sul-razzismo/

[13] Rivera, A. (2011) 'Due anni di scena razzista in Italia. Protagonisti e comprimari, vittime e ribelli' ['Two years of racism in Italy. Main actors and secondary players, victims and rebels'], *Cronache di ordinario razzismo* [*Chronicles of ordinary racism*], Rome: Edizioni dell'Asino.

[14] The metalworkers' trade union of the left.

[15] Longhi, V. (2008) 'La nostra Africa, tra Usa e Ghana' ['Our Africa, between the USA and Ghana', *Il Manifesto*, 11 November.

[16] Corriere.it (2008) 'Castelvolturno, rivolta degli immigrati dopo la strage di camorra' ['Castel Volturno, revolt of the immigrants after the massacre by the Camorra'], 19 September.

[17] Mangano, A. (2009) *Gli africani salveranno Rosarno* [*The Africans will save Rosarno*], terrelibere.org

[18] RaiNews24.it (2010) 'Caccia al nero in Rosarno' ['Hunting blacks in Rosarno'], 9 January (www.rainews24.rai.it/it/news.php?newsid=136613).

[19] Longhi, V. (2010) 'Italy: a country united by racism', *The Guardian*, 10 January (www.guardian.co.uk/commentisfree/2010/jan/10/italy-human-rights).

[20] Saviano, R. (2010) 'Italy's African heroes', *The New York Times*, 24 January (www.nytimes.com/2010/01/25/opinion/25saviano.html).

[21] Colombo, A. and Sciortino, G. (2004) *Gli immigrati in Italia* [*Immigrants in Italy*], Bologna: Il Mulino, p 25.

[22] The government had strongly supported the adoption of this Convention because Italy had a long history of emigration with many workers abroad who had been and were still subject to discrimination.

[23] Law 39 of 1990, known as the Martelli law after the name of the then Minister for Internal Affairs, the socialist Claudio Martelli.

[24] In 2011 Italian citizens resident abroad exceeded four million, almost as numerous as migrants without citizenship resident in Italy.

[25] Law No 40, 6 March 1998, 'Disciplina dell'immigrazione e norme sulla condizione dello straniero' ['Regulation of immigration and the status of aliens', known as the Turco-Napolitano law from the names of the two ministers signing it, Livia Turco and Giorgio Napolitano of the centre left (www.camera.it/parlam/leggi/98040l.htm).

[26] Law No 189, 30 July 2002, 'Modifica alla normativa in materia di immigrazione e di asilo' ['Changing the rules on immigration and asylum'] (www.camera.it/parlam/leggi/02189l.htm).

[27] Colombo and Sciortino, op cit.

[28] Italian regulations, UNHCR (www.unhcr.it/news/dir/59/la-normativa-italiana.html).

[29] Ministry for Employment (2011) 'L'immigrazione per lavoro in Italia: evoluzione e prospettive' ['Labour immigration in Italy: evolution and

perspectives'], p XXII (www.lavoro.gov.it/NR/rdonlyres/A8D198AF-983E-459F-9CD1-A59C14C0DEA9/0/Rapporto_Immigrazione_2011.pdf).

[30] *Corriere della Sera* (2009) 'La crescita degli immigrati non toglie lavoro agli italiani' ['The growth of immigrants does not mean no work for Italians'], 18 August (www.corriere.it/economia/09_agosto_18/lavoro_immigrati_togliere_9e9c20fa-8be8-11de-a273-00144f02aabc.shtml).

[31] Ambrosini, M. (2005) *Sociologia delle migrazioni* [*The sociology of migration*], Bologna: Il Mulino.

[32] Caritas Migrantes (2011) *Dossier statistico immigrazione 2011* [*Statistics on immigration 2011*], 21st report, Rome: Idos.

[33] Polchi, V. (2011) 'Gli immigrati danno più di quanto ricevono. Ecco i dati Inps raccolti e diffusi dalla Caritas' ['Immigrants make more than they receive. Data collected by INPS and disseminated by Caritas'], *La Repubblica*, 9 June (www.repubblica.it/solidarieta/immigrazione/2011/06/09/news/immigrazione_e_inpsvladimiro_polchi-17448178/).

[34] *Corriere della Sera* (2009) 'Maroni: "Cattivi contro i clandestini"' ['Maroni, "harsh with the clandestines"'], 2 February (www.corriere.it/politica/09_febbraio_02/maroni_immigrazione_clandestina_cattivi_6cdc5e96-f155-11dd-b48f-00144f02aabc.shtml).

[35] *Corriere della Sera* (2009) 'Il gran finale della campagna del Pdl Berlusconi: "Milano sembra africana"' ['The grand finale of the PDL campaign for Berlusconi:"Milan appears to be African"'], 4 June (www.corriere.it/politica/speciali/2009/elezioni/notizie/bossi_berlusconi_chiusura_campagna_elettorale_72a37414-5130-11de-9de2-00144f02aabc.shtml).

[36] Galossi, E. (2008) *Immigrazione e sindacato* [*Immigration and unions*], 5th report of IRES, Rome: Ediesse.

[37] Caritas Migrantes, op cit.

[38] Galossi, op cit, p 154.

[39] Ministry for the Interior (2010) *Regulations on the security package and associated matters* (updated on 17 March).

[40] Boldrini, L. (2012) 'A ruling for the future', Blog 'Popoli in fuga', Repubblica.it, 23 February (http://boldrini.blogautore.repubblica.it/2012/02/una-sentenza-per-il-futuro/).

[41] Interview, 14 October 2010.

[42] Veneto CISL (2010) 'Sciopero degli immigrati. Stranieri strumentalizzati' ['Immigrants' strike. Foreigners exploited', 24 February, Press release

(www.cislveneto.it/Rassegna-stampa-Veneto/Sciopero-degli-immigrati.-Stranieri-strumentalizzati).

[43] Farolfi, S. (2010) 'Primo marzo, un giorno senza migranti' ['First of March, a day without migrants'], *Il Manifesto*, 12 January.

[44] Greco, D. (2010) 'Immigrati e sindacati, un problema c'è' ['Immigrants and unions, there is a problem', *Liberazione*, 22 January.

[45] See http://primomarzo2010.blogspot.com/

[46] Il Sole 24 ore (2011) 'Napolitano: diritto di cittadinanza a figli di immigrati nati in Italia. Da Maroni netto no a "ius soli"' ['Napolitano: right of citizenship for children of immigrants born in Italy'], 22 November (www.ilsole24ore.com/art/notizie/2011-11-22/napolitano-facile-confronto-forze-120311.shtml?uuid=AaVXybNE).

[47] Rights for All (2010) 'Ancora multe razziste contro i giocatori di cricket' ['Racist fines continue against cricket players'], 4 May (http://dirittipertutti.gnumerica.org/2010/05/04/multe-razziste-contro-giocatori-di-cricket/).

[48] De Riccardis, S. (2009, 18 November) 'Un bianco Natale senza immigrati. Per le feste il comune caccia i clandestini' ['A white Christmas without immigrants. Hunting illegal immigrants for the holidays'], *La Repubblica*, 18 November (www.repubblica.it/2009/11/sezioni/cronaca/natale-a-coccaglio/natale-a-coccaglio/natale-a-coccaglio.html).

[49] *Corriere della Sera* (2011) 'Bonus bebè negato agli stranieri: condannato il comune leghista di Adro' ['Baby bonus denied to foreigners: Condemned, the League town of Adro'], 16 December (Brescia edn) (http://brescia.corriere.it/brescia/notizie/cronaca/11_dicembre_16/adro-condanna-1902561235645.shtml).

[50] UNAR (2011) 'Town Council of Gavardo (BS): UNAR, "Quell'ordinanza è discriminatoria"', 8 October, News (www.unar.it).

[51] Interview, 14 October 2010.

[52] Interview, 14 October 2010.

[53] Berizzi, P. and de Giorgio, T. (2010) 'Brescia, gli immigrati scendono dalla gru "Ora un tavolo sulle truffe per i permessi"' ['Brescia, migrants come down from the crane "Time to negotiate on the scam of permits"'], *La Repubblica*, 15 November (http://milano.repubblica.it/cronaca/2010/11/15/news/gli_immigrati_scendono_dalla_gru_dopo_una_protesta_lunga_16_giorni-9152398/).

[54] Berruto, S. (2011) 'Accolto il ricorso di Mohamed El Haga' ['Mohamed El Haga appeal upheld'], Blog by Silvia Berruto, 30 March (http://silviaberruto. wordpress.com/2011/03/30/accolto-il-ricorso-di-mohamed-el-haga/).

[55] Ciamponi, M. and Giovannini, E. (2011) 'Sopra e sotto la torre, immigrati e lavoro al Nord' ['Above and below the tower, immigants and employment in the north'], Tre soldi, Radio Tre, 17-21 October.

[56] Cosentino, R. (2011) 'Caporalato, Cgil: "Punire le aziende e tutelare i lavoratori che denunciano"' ['Illegal hiring, CGIL: "punish the companies and protect the workers who denounce them"'], Redattore Sociale, 16 November.

[57] Cosentino, ibid.

[58] Leongrande, A. (2008) Uomini e caporali [Men and corporals], Milan: Mondadori.

[59] Interview, 25 November 2011.

[60] The project consists of setting up a voluntary reception camp directed towards seasonal workers in Nardò from 15 June to 30 August (http:// brigatesolidarietaattiva.blogspot.com/p/ingaggiami-contro-il-lavoro-nero-campo.html).

[61] Interview, 25 November 2011.

[62] Spagnolo, C. (2011) 'Motta: "Dai migranti un esempio hanno il coraggio di denunciare"' ['Motta: "Migrants give an example of the courage to denounce"'], La Repubblica, 7 August (http://bari.repubblica.it/ cronaca/2011/08/07/news/motta_dai_migranti_un_esempio_hanno_il_ coraggio_di_denunciare-20124793/).

[63] The crime of acting as an illegal middleman and exploiting labour became part of the Criminal Code with article 12 of Decree Law No 138 of 13 August 2011. This replacement for article 603bis of the Criminal Code punishes anyone carrying out an activity 'organised using middlemen, recruiting manpower or organising work activity characterised by exploitation, by means of violence, threats or intimidation, taking advantage of the needy situation of workers' with imprisonment for five to eight years and a fine of €1,000 to €2,000 for every worker recruited, plus additional penalties'.

[64] Loiero, V. (2012) 'Viaggio a Rosarno due anni dopo' ['Return to Rosarno, two years on'], 9 January (www.zoomsud.it).

[65] Loiero, ibid.

[66] Mangano, A. (2010) 'Castel Volturno. Gli africani hanno scioperato per noi' ['Castel Volturno. The Africans have been on strike for us'], 9 October, terrelibere.org (www.terrelibere.org/castel-volturno-gli-africani-hanno-scioperato-per-noi).

Chapter 5

[1] Bertelsmann Stiftung and Migration Policy Institute (eds) (2012) *Improving the governance of international migration*, Washington, DC: Transatlantic Council on Migration.

[2] Chamie, J. and Mirkin, B. (2009) *Who's afraid of international migration in the United Nations?*, 27 April, New York: Center for Migration Studies.

[3] See www.globalmigrationgroup.org/

[4] ILO (International Labour Organization) (nd) 'Decent work agenda' (www.ilo.org/global/about-the-ilo/decent-work-agenda/lang--en/index.htm).

[5] See www.gfmd.org/

[6] ITUC News (2010) 'Unions demand rights for migrant workers at Global Forum', 10 November (www.ituc-csi.org/unions-demand-rights-for-migrant.html).

[7] UN (United Nations), Department of Economic and Social Affairs, Population Division (2011) *Trends in international migrant stock: Migrants by age and sex*, UN database, POP/DB/MIG/Stock/Rev.2011.

[8] ILO (International Labour Organization) (2010) *International labour migration: A rights-based approach*, Geneva.

[9] IOM (International Organization for Migration) (2008) *Addressing mixed migration flows*, Geneva.

[10] Ambrosini, M. (2005) *Sociologia delle migrazioni* [*The sociology of migration*], Bologna: Il Mulino, p 133.

[11] Based on the theory of dependence, which was drawn up in the 1960s with reference to Latin American countries, the world economy is structured according to an unequal design, which assigns a peripheral role to non-developed countries in the production of raw materials with low added value, while fundamental decisions are made by central countries, which are assigned industrial production with high added value.

[12] Koser, K. (2007) *International migrations*, Oxford: Oxford University Press.

[13] According to the parameters of the UN, the Index is obtained with an average from GDP per capita, life expectancy and level of education.

[14] Piore, M. (1979) *Birds of passage: Migrant labor and industrial societies*, Cambridge: Cambridge University Press.

[15] Koser, op cit.

[16] Koser, ibid.

[17] Ambrosini, op cit, p 133.

[18] Melotti, U. (2004) *Migrazioni internazionali, globalizzazione e culture politiche* [*International migration, globalisation and political culture*], Milan: Bruno Mondadori.

[19] Koser, op cit.

[20] Melotti, op cit.

[21] ILO (International Labour Organization) (2010) *International labour migration: A rights-based approach*, Geneva.

[22] World Bank (2011) *The migration and remittances factbook*, Washington, DC: World Bank.

[23] World Bank, ibid.

[24] Koser, op cit.

[25] Levitt, P. and Lamba-Nieves, D. (2011) 'Social remittances reconsidered', *Journal of Ethnic and Migration Studies*, vol 37, no 1, pp 1-22.

[26] Koser, op cit.

[27] Erhenreich, B. (2004) *Donne globali* [*Global women*], Milan: Feltrinelli.

[28] OHCHR (Office of the High Commissioner for Human Rights) (1990) *International Convention on the Protection of the Rights of All Migrant Workers and Members of Their Families* (www2.ohchr.org/english/law/cmw.htm).

[29] At the beginning of 2012 the countries that had ratified it were: Albania, Argentina, Algeria, Azerbaijan, Bangladesh, Belize, Bolivia, Bosnia Herzegovina, Burkina Faso, Cape Verde, Chile, Colombia, East Timor, Ecuador, Egypt, El Salvador, Ghana, Jamaica, Guatemala, Guyana, Guinea, Honduras, Kyrgyzstan, Lesotho, Libya, Mali, Mauritania, Mexico, Morocco, Nicaragua, Niger, Nigeria, Paraguay, Peru, Philippines, Rwanda, Senegal, Seychelles, Sri Lanka, Saint Vincent and Grenadine, Syria, Tagikistan, West Timor, Turkey, Uganda and Uruguay.

[30] Ban Ki-Moon, General Secretary of the UN (United Nations) (2010) Speech to the Council of Europe, 19 October (www.un.org/sg/statements/?nid=4862).

[31] de Guchteneire, P. and Pécoud, A. (2009) *Migration and human rights*, Cambridge: Unesco Publishing/Cambridge University Press.

[32] de Guchteneire and Pécoud, ibid.

[33] Böhning, R. (1991) 'The ILO and the new UN Convention on Migrant Workers: the past and the future', *International Migration Review*, vol 25, no 4, pp 698-709.

[34] ILO (International Labour Organization) (nd) 'Labour standards' (www.ilo.org/global/standards/lang--en/index.htm).

[35] ILO (International Labour Organization) (nd) 'Labour migration' (www.ilo.org/global/topics/labour-migration/lang--en/index.htm).

[36] ILO (International Labour Organization) (2006) *Multilateral framework on labour migration*, Geneva.

[37] Europa.eu (2011) 'A Single Permit and a clear set of rights for legal migrant workers', 13 December (http://europa.eu/rapid/pressReleasesAction.do?reference=MEMO/11/901&format=HTML&aged=0&language=EN&guiLanguage=en).

[38] Associated Press (2011) 'EU: more migrants needed to fill jobs of future', 18 November.

[39] Europa.eu (2009) 'Entry and residence of highly qualified workers (EU Blue Card)', 18 August (http://europa.eu/legislation_summaries/internal_market/living_and_working_in_the_internal_market/l14573_en.htm).

[40] Ambrosini, op cit, p 133.

[41] Melotti, op cit.

[42] Europa.eu (2011) 'A common immigration policy for Europe', 16 May, Summary of EU legislation (http://europa.eu/legislation_summaries/justice_freedom_security/free_movement_of_persons_asylum_immigration/jl0001_en.htm).

[43] Cantaro, A. (2007) *Il diritto dimenticato* [*Forgotten rights*], Turin: Giappichelli Editore.

[44] Eur-Lex (2005) 'Green Paper on an EU approach to managing economic migration', 11 January (http://eur-lex.europa.eu/LexUriServ/LexUriServ.do?uri=CELEX:52004DC0811:EN:HTML).

[45] Ambrosini, op cit, p 133.

[46] Longhi, V. (2009) 'E con la crisi vengono allontanati anche gli immigrati regolari' ['And with the crisis, legal immigrants are also removed'], *La Repubblica*, 11 May (www.repubblica.it/2009/05/sezioni/cronaca/immigrati-7/crisi-esplusioni/crisi-esplusioni.html).

[47] IOM (International Organization for Migration) (2011) *Migration and the economic crisis: Implications for policy in the European Union*, Geneva.

[48] Tanner, A. (2009) 'The global recession and African migration: A pending crisis', *The Harvard International Review* (http://hir.harvard.edu/the-global-recession-and-african-migration).

[49] Quatremer, J. (2011) 'Tunisie, Egypte: l'Union dans le mauvais tempo' ['Tunisia, Egypt: The Union in a bad time'], *Libération*, 17 February (www. liberation.fr/monde/01012320510-tunisie-egypte-l-union-dans-le-mauvais-tempo).

[50] Longhi, V. (2011) 'Is EU serious about supporting human rights across north Africa?', *The Guardian*, 25 February (www.guardian.co.uk/global-development/poverty-matters/2011/feb/25/libya-eu-human-rights-response).

[51] *The Economist* (2011) 'The magic of diasporas', 19 November.

[52] Sombart, W. (1967) *Il capitalismo modern* [*Modern capitalism*], Turin: Utet.

[53] *The Economist*, op cit.

[54] Barberis, E. (2008) *Imprenditori immigrati* [*Immigrant entrepreneurs*], Rome: Ediesse.

[55] University of Cambridge (2011) *Digital diasporas: Migration, ICTs and transnationalism*, 13 January.

[56] Diminescu, D. (2011) 'Connected migrants: Rethinking the sociology of migrations', in *Digital diasporas: Migration, ICTs and transnationalism*, University of Cambridge.

[57] Horst, H. (2011) 'Conceptualizing digital diasporas', in *Digital diasporas: Migration, ICTs and transnationalism*, University of Cambridge.

[58] Gillespie, M. (2011) 'Digital diasporas and diplomatic imperatives at the BBC World Service', in *Digital diasporas: Migration, ICTs and transnationalism*, University of Cambridge.

[59] Brighenti, A.M. (2009) *Territori migrant* [*Migrant territory*], Verona: Ombre Corte.

[60] Tapscott, D. (2009) *Growing up digital*, New York: McGraw-Hill Companies.

[61] Sassen, S. (1988) *The mobility of labour and capital: A study in international investment and labour flow*, Cambridge: Cambridge University Press.

[62] Sassen, S. (1999) *Migranti, coloni, rifugiati* [*Migrants, colonists, refugees*], Milan: Feltrinelli.

[63] Bosniak, L. (2000) 'Citizenship denationalized', *Indiana Journal of Global Law Studies*, vol 7.

[64] Maxwell, R. (2010) 'Evaluating migrant integration: political attitudes across generations in Europe', *International Migration Review*, vol 44, no 1.

[65] Gropas, R. (2009) 'Immigrants and political rights', *The Bridge, a Quarterly Review on European Integration* (www.bridge-mag.com/index.

php?option=com_content&view=article&id=186:immigrants-and-political-rights&catid=17:dialogue-2007&Itemid=22).

[66] Marshall, T.H. (1950) *Citizenship and social class and other essays*, Cambridge: Cambridge University Press.

[67] Sassen, S. (2006) *Territory, authority, rights. From Medieval to global assemblages*, Princeton, NJ: Princeton University Press.

[68] Lo Faro, A. (1997) 'Immigrazione, lavoro, cittadinanza' ['Immigration, work, citizenship'], *Giornale di diritto del lavoro e di relazioni industriali*, Pamphlet 76.

Index

Note: The following abbreviation has been used: *n* = note